THE
Endurance
L E A D E R

THE

Endurance
LE▲DER

Leadership Longevity
In A Fast-Paced World

ANN BOWERS-EVANGELISTA

INDIE BOOKS
INTERNATIONAL

For Dave
LOML, you are always and forever my inspiration.
Thank you for believing in me, challenging me,
and making me pizza.

The Endurance LEADER

Leadership Longevity In A Fast-Paced World

Use of Pseudonyms and Real Names
Throughout this book, I have used pseudonyms to protect the anonymity of individuals. Some characters are indicated by first name only. Where first and last names are listed, I have received permission from these individuals to use their real names. I am grateful for their willingness to be a part of this work.

ISBN-13: 978-1-957651-95-8
Library of Congress Control Number: 2024920485

Designed by Melissa Farr, Back Porch Creative, LLC

INDIE BOOKS INTERNATIONAL®, INC.
2511 WOODLANDS WAY
OCEANSIDE, CA 92054
www.indiebooksintl.com

Table Of Contents

Foreword
by Dr. Marshall Goldsmith

The Endurance Leader by Ann Bowers-Evangelista offers a groundbreaking leadership approach that nails the very essence of what I speak about in my book *The Earned Life* that our lives only make sense when we are aligned with our greater purpose. Ann's four-part Endurance Leader model not only helps leaders develop the right mindset to live their purpose but also how to build the discipline, skills, and support structures to help them lead successfully with energy, resilience, and meaning for decades.

Do you ever wish you didn't feel like you were sprinting a marathon every day? Do you ever wonder how you'll keep up your energy to lead for the next twenty to thirty years? Ann's extensive research and interviews with successful long-term leaders and endurance athletes, as well as her unique lens as a twenty-five-plus year business psychologist, Ironman triathlete, and marathon runner, ground *The Endurance Leader* in theory and practical realities. Ann shows how, when you start putting aside the 'tyranny of the urgent' to focus your mindset and actions like an endurance athlete, you are less likely to experience the ongoing stress, anxiety, burnout, and work dissatisfaction that are all too common in today's business climate.

This book isn't about quick wins; it's a masterclass in building leadership that stands the test of time. Ann's model is a compass that guides leaders through the labyrinth of their leadership journey, stressing the importance of mindset, discipline, skill, and support. This is the very fabric of a leadership capable of withstanding the relentless marathon of today's demanding business world.

Chapter by chapter, Ann weaves together the stories of everyday leaders and extraordinary athletes to show how *The Endurance Leader* model really works. Providing real-world coaching questions and training plans, she helps you apply these concepts in practical ways. You don't need to be an Ironman triathlete to make these concepts work; you only need a heart to live your ultimate purpose and the willingness to reach for fuller, longer-lasting effectiveness.

Each chapter feels like a personal coaching session, full of stories and strategies that'll make you nod in recognition and scribble notes in the margins. Ann offers actionable coaching tools and developmental plans, extending an invitation to transcend short-term gratifications for a lasting impact. It's for anyone who's tired of the daily grind and looking for more—more depth, more satisfaction, more longevity in their leadership journey. This is a journey of transformation, not just for the elite, but for any leader seeking to cultivate a legacy of meaningful influence.

Ann's work is a testament to the power of perseverance and the pursuit of excellence. Embrace this book as a mentor for your leadership growth—a guide that your future self will regard with pride and gratitude. It's a clarion call to leaders: to craft a narrative of leadership that's not just effective for today but one that you can be proud of for a lifetime.

Life is good.

Dr. Marshall Goldsmith is the *Thinkers50* #1 Executive Coach and New York Times bestselling author of *The Earned Life, Triggers,* and *What Got You Here Won't Get You There.*

Preface

▬▬ ▬▬ ▬▬ ▬▬ ▬▬ ▬▬

We are different, in essence, from other [people].
If you want to win something, run 100 meters.
If you want to experience something, run a marathon.
Emil Zatopek

The Big Question

What do you think? Is life (and leadership) a marathon or a series of sprints?

We live in an era that hails the temporal. We are regularly deluged with people celebrating their most recent victory, whether finishing a local 5K run or announcing quarterly profits on a shareholder call. Pressures for quick wins seem ever-increasing in business: leaders are continually pushed to do more, go faster, and use fewer resources.

In my coaching and consulting practice, I often encounter leaders who feel they are running as fast as possible to deliver impressive results but are barely keeping up. They think doing *more* is the only way to advance in their careers. They try to manage unrelenting expectations by working more hours or pushing their team harder.

While these solutions are sensible, they tend to be shortsighted. Often, they result in fatigue, burnout, stress, and relationship challenges. One female leader recently said, "I can't keep up with all the pressures and responsibilities; I constantly feel like I'm failing at home and work." This might feel like sprinting a marathon, as leaders try their hardest to keep up a blistering pace but, ultimately, cannot sustain it.

Are you looking instead to build leadership that remains resilient in the face of adversity, helps you manage setbacks, and compels you to perform at your absolute best, professionally and personally, for years to come? Do you desire to create a leadership legacy that will inspire your contemporaries and future generations? If so, the endurance leader model can help you achieve it.

Reality Check

Let's experiment to determine where you are in your endurance leadership journey. Read the two lists below and determine which one has more statements that resonate with you. You may find yourself in both camps, but one may ring truer for you than the other.

Group 1 Statements

- I need to be better at prioritization and time management.
- I just want things to slow down so I can get organized.
- I want to be the best _____ in the company (salesperson/operations leader/etc.).
- I need my team to stop fighting with each other.
- I wish the company would just get rid of that person.
- I want to double my salary in the next five years.
- I only need to finish this one thing _____ (email/project task/ checklist), and I can get on with my more important tasks.

Group 2 Statements

- I want my work to reflect my commitment to serving others and showing my daughters what working moms can do.
- My goal is to be known as the best boss my team has ever had.
- Our team has some challenging personalities, but we can sort through our differences over time.
- I want to keep a solid balance between my work and family, allowing me to continue loving what I do in and out of the office.
- I want to lead with greater resiliency to continue to perform even when things are tough.

Be honest; where did you find yourself? If you resonated primarily with Group 1 statements, you may be thinking like a sprinter. While you may meet many short-term goals, you may have difficulty finding the energy and resources to keep your leadership strong over a lifetime. If you find yourself more aligned with Group 2 statements, you may already be thinking like an endurance leader. You recognize the need for a long-term perspective and a deep connection with what matters to keep you going. In either group, you may find the frameworks and strategies in this book useful.

Endurance And Everyday People

Besides spending twenty-five years advising top leaders and executives on strategies to build long-term success, I am an endurance athlete. I have completed over sixty endurance races, including a full Ironman race (which is comprised of a 2.4-mile swim, 112-mile bike, and a 26.2-mile run) and several half-Ironman races (half those distances). I have also enjoyed working with, training alongside, and observing a legion of endurance athletes. As my experience in consulting and endurance sports grew, their relationship became ever more apparent. And I realized that leaders could benefit from leveraging endurance qualities to build their long-term leadership success.

Like well-known, long-term successful leaders, professional endurance athletes are a rare breed. Most people competing in endurance races are not elite athletes; they are *everyday people* like you and me. We comprise 99 percent of entrants in any endurance event. We enter long, grueling races not with the expectation that we will win the event but rather for the opportunity to challenge ourselves, see what is possible, and possibly find the best version of ourselves.

Leadership is the same: most leaders will not be hailed in *Harvard Business Review* or praised on the cover of the *Wall Street Journal*. But like endurance athletes, endurance leaders are *everyday people* seeking to improve their impact. Their resources and tools may not be the most sophisticated, and they probably won't have eight hours a day to dedicate to improving their leadership. But, with the right mindset, heart, determination, and support, they can create a lasting impact for themselves and their families. This book is for *everyday people*.

The endurance leader model is not about *elite* performance but about *lasting* performance. It is about cultivating ways of thinking, acting, and engaging that are satisfying and sustainable. It is not about winning races but the strategies to repeatedly get you across the finish line. And no one understands the requirements of that success better than the endurance athlete.

I started the book by asking if life (and leadership) is a marathon or a series of sprints. Which would you pick? Which do you think I would pick? Spoiler alert: My answer is both. I believe longevity in life and leadership requires a series of sprints within a marathon. My rationale will become clearer as you read on.

Preparing For This Book

If you feel motivated to read this book, here are a few pieces of advice as your endurance leader coach:

- *Decide if the book is for you.* You may find yourself looking for a ready-made prescription or tools and tricks to help you deliver in the face of overwhelming demands. Indeed, there are plenty of old-school and tech-intensive resources to help you manage your email, build your presentation skills, or network like a pro. This book is not one of them, however. If your goal is cultivating a framework and roadmap to sustainable leadership success across your lifetime, this book is for you.

- *The endurance leader model is a personal leadership journey.* There are thousands of leadership books focusing on leading others, leading teams, and leading organizations. The endurance leader model focuses squarely on the leading self domain (see Figure 1). To succeed in those other domains, we must first focus on developing our mindset and personal self-management practices to ensure we are true to ourselves. Without that, we will forever depend on others to anchor our activities and experiences in meaning, which is a risky proposition at best and disastrous at worst. Investing in the endurance leader concept means investing in yourself so that you may serve others most effectively.

Figure 1: The Five Levels of Leadership[1]

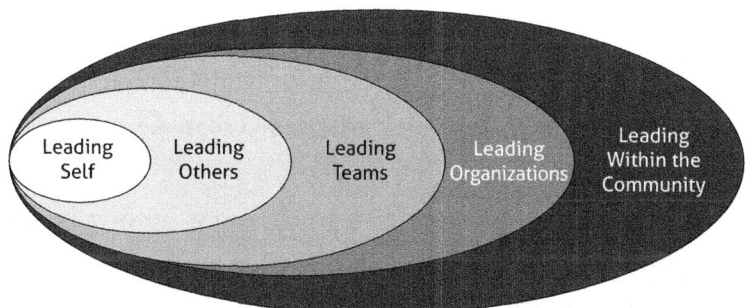

- *This book is designed for everyday leaders, not those aspiring to elite status.* The ideal reader is probably in the middle stages of leadership. They are still developing the strategies and solutions to master their leadership craft. That does not mean expert or elite leaders cannot benefit from the ideas here; they may find the frameworks helpful if they find themselves stuck, burned out, or trying to reignite their motivation for the next career phase. But if you are looking for strategies to help you get promoted, accelerate up the success ladder quickly, or earn your place in the rarified air of some status position, this may not be the book for you.

- *You do not need to be an athlete to benefit from reading this.* You can know nothing about sports or even dislike them (I won't tell). But you might find it valuable if you have marveled at the incredible capacities of leaders who have led successfully for decades and seem to love doing it. You will meet several of them in this book. And if you are an endurance athlete or a long-time sports performer, you will find a natural home here.

- *Treat it as a type of playbook.* Each chapter's end will have opportunities for self-reflection (Coach's Questions) and action (Training Plan). You are encouraged to write in it, scribble, doodle, or think on paper. Really use it!

- *There are many resources to substantiate the book's premises and help you.* Leverage these to help you become an endurance leader.

- *Challenge the content.* Nothing is as fun as a healthy skeptic with a sense of humor. Challenge the assumptions and compare them to your own experience. You will get much more out of it.

- *Have fun with it.* This book is intended to make you a stronger and more effective leader—for longer. Yes, it's work, but don't be afraid to try new things, laugh at yourself, screw up royally sometimes. If building long-term success isn't fun, we are doing something seriously wrong.

I look forward to this journey with you and will be here every step of the way.

Ann B-E
Washington, D.C.

PART I

The Endurance Leader Model

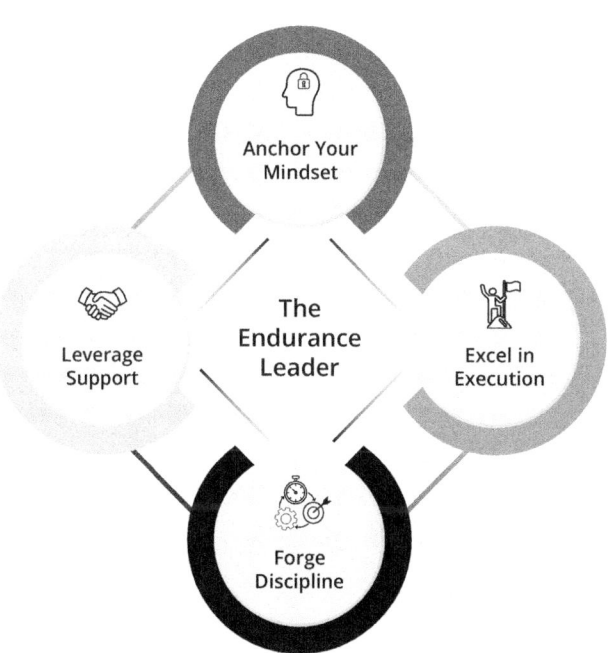

Chapter 1

The Endurance Leader

You will make better decisions once you begin thinking long-term rather than short-term.
ADAM SMITH

The Need For Endurance In Leadership

"I just don't know how long I can do this." Preethi and I weren't far into our coaching conversation before she slumped in her chair, rubbed her weary eyes, and made this sobering declaration. As vice president of operations at a large equipment manufacturing company, she had been sitting at her desk since 3:30 a.m. and looked exhausted and beleaguered. She had been working twelve-hour days for months, navigating new and unprecedented realities in her business, prompted by global health and economic crises.

Ensuring employees and facilities were safe while maintaining production volume and low overhead costs was a daily challenge. Considered essential workers during a major public health crisis, Preethi and most of her staff came into the office every day while many others in her company worked from home. This created additional stress on her and her team. Meanwhile, her children had shifted to virtual school, and Preethi had to quickly pivot to find childcare when few people wanted to be in others' homes. It seemed there was a fresh perdition arising with every passing day.

When I began coaching Preethi a few months prior, we'd built her strategic thinking and delegation skills. However, for several weeks before this conversation, much of her energy was spent trying to hold her head above water. She felt overwhelmed, stressed, and unsure of how to forge ahead. With almost no time to rest and reflect, she found it hard to plan much further than one to two days, let alone meet our development objectives. More than once, Preethi had said, "I feel like I'm in a constant sprint."

The Challenge Of The Constant Sprint

Does this sound familiar? Do you feel like you've been sprinting a marathon for the past few months (or years)? With business demands unrelenting, change happening faster than ever, and global issues fundamentally altering how we live, many people feel they are struggling to stay upright. And the impact is taking a massive toll on our physical, emotional, and mental health.

Some alarming statistics:

From The 2023 American Psychological Association's 2023 *Stress in America* survey:[2]

- Chronic illness in the US increased from 48 percent in 2019 to 58 percent in 2023 among adults ages 35–44. This group also experienced the highest increase in mental health diagnoses, from 31 percent to 45 percent.
- Adults ages 18–34 had the highest rate of mental illness in 2023, at 50 percent (in case math isn't your strong subject, it means that *one in every two adults* in this age range carries a mental illness diagnosis).
- "Women report feeling stressed, misunderstood, and alone at higher rates than men."[3]

- "Gen Z adults and younger millennials are 'completely overwhelmed' by stress."[4]

From the Gallup organization's December 2023 findings:[5]

- Daily stress among employees globally remained stubbornly high through 2022, with 52 percent of employees in the US and Canada reporting they experienced a lot of stress the previous day.
- Managers, constantly trying to do more with less and manage continually changing priorities, are more likely to be disengaged, burned out, and job hunting than nonmanagers. These statistics are signs of a workforce experiencing prolonged stress and increased risk of depression, anxiety, or other mental health challenges.

Gallup's meta-analytic study of its Q12 engagement tool stated, "The 2020 meta-analysis verified once again that employee engagement relates to each of the eleven performance outcomes studied. Gallup also finds that the strong correlations between engagement and performance are highly consistent across different organizations from diverse industries and regions of the world." They also consistently found that companies with high employee engagement have higher earnings per share.[6] In other words, employees who are more engaged perform better.

Even a company that doesn't prioritize wellness or engagement might want to stand up and take notice. However, most organizations find it challenging to shift their expectations to reward long-term thinking, leading, and acting because the business climate incentivizes short-term profitability. With the accelerated pace of change in every industry, organizations must move faster and work harder to keep pace.

This brings us back to Preethi. Preethi's company has not lessened its expectations of her and her team. Pressures increased as change and uncertainty multiplied. Her boss, while sympathetic, was not able to do much to alter the organization's expectations. So, what's Preethi to do? Just grit her teeth, hold her breath, and hope the continued sprinting will pay off? As I watched her in this uncomfortable state, I knew that would never result in an optimal outcome. Instead, Preethi needed a longer-term perspective that could help her see beyond her immediate challenges. She needed something that would inspire her, compel her to stand firm amid difficulty, and ultimately help her persevere in achieving what is deeply important to her. We will check in with Preethi and her Endurance Leader journey later.

Endurance Leaders And Endurance Athletes

Over my career, I've worked with leaders from virtually every walk of life—young and old, novice and veteran, private and nonprofit—and from every race, color, gender identification, and many countries of origin. I've observed that some are better than others at maintaining a long-term vision and commitment, even in the face of tremendous obstacles. I call these people *endurance leaders* because they share essential qualities with *endurance athletes*. Both build a specific way of thinking, a core sense of discipline, and a commitment to execution that drives long-term leadership success. Don't get me wrong; they must be successful in the short term to have a shot at making those long-term impacts. However, they are unique among their colleagues for their disciplined and focused approach to leadership anchored in something beyond the moment.

Let me illustrate with two examples: an endurance athlete and an endurance leader. Can you spot the similarities?

In 1986, eighteen-year-old Scott Rigsby underwent a life-changing event. In a highway sideswipe, Rigsby was pulled from the pickup bed where he'd been sitting and dragged over 300 feet underneath a three-ton semi tractor trailer. He survived, but barely. Rigsby lost one of his legs and had over twenty-six surgeries in the first year to repair the other. Within a few years, his remaining leg was so painful that he decided to amputate it too. For years, Rigsby struggled to find purpose and meaning in his life. Seeing his future altered forever, he had neither the mindset nor discipline to face the adversity in front of him. He went through almost two decades of anger and grief, using alcohol, drugs, and violence as a result. He battled depression, at times contemplating suicide.

Around 2005, Rigsby went through life-changing experiences that altered his mindset. He also took up the endurance sport of triathlon, which requires swimming, biking, and running. Rigsby learned to swim without legs and used modifications to help him cycle and run. In 2007, Scott became the first double amputee to complete the Ironman World Championship race in Kona, Hawaii. The race is one of the most difficult athletic feats in the world, requiring participants to swim in rough waters, bicycle through high winds in the island's lava fields, and then run in temperatures often well above ninety degrees Fahrenheit. The task is arduous for anyone, but for Rigsby, the obstacles were tremendous: for example, with three miles left to run, sweat pooled in his prosthetic legs, ripping the skin off Rigsby's legs. "How do you push through that kind of pain when you're that close to your finish line?" he asked a reporter in an interview. "You won't. You'll give up, you'll quit—if you're not playing a role in a bigger story."[7]

Rigsby was completing the race for a bigger story: inspiring other amputees and wounded military members. He was also doing it for his older brother, who was born with disabilities. He established a nonprofit, The Scott Rigsby Foundation, which helped other amputees achieve extraordinary goals. His mindset, determination, and strength of character helped him achieve goals that many nondisabled people could never achieve. That is an endurance athlete!

My friend Ji-Ho (Jimmy) has been a successful executive for decades. Starting his career in finance, he rose from accountant to comptroller to CFO and, eventually, to CEO. In a new CEO opportunity, Jimmy was challenged to build a new hospital from the ground up. Some team members privately voiced concerns about his ability to lead a long-term, complex, high-stakes project. However, after learning that Jimmy was also an ultramarathon runner, one team member said, "Well, we have nothing to worry about. We'll be fine."

Indeed, Jimmy and his team built a world-class hospital facility, ranking in the top ten in its class two years after opening its doors. However, the project was not without its challenges: Construction delays, high-level staff changes, and technological challenges plagued the project. Jimmy had many sleepless nights. But he continued to push the project forward, dig deep when things were tough, and promulgate the vision he and the hospital board had for a life-changing institution for thousands of children. He held fast to his true mission and achieved—in fact, exceeded—the goal.

In an interview, Jimmy told me: "A project of that significance [the hospital] is like training for a marathon: you must have the vision, to plan it, and part of the goal then is never to give up. It's the ID I wear on my wrist and my shoelaces, 'Never give up.'"[8]

Do you find similarities between these stories? While Jimmy's story isn't as dramatic as Rigsby's, you can bet the financial, time, and human investments created an Ironman-type intensity for him. In both cases, you see people who delivered incredible results despite daunting challenges and obstacles. They were inspired and motivated by things beyond the moment, and they could call upon those motivators at their darkest hours to help them push back pain, frustration, and the desire to give up.

Endurance And The Everyday Leader

You may think, "I don't have much in common with Scott Rigsby or Jimmy." Indeed, these are impressive individuals who have been superstars in their areas of expertise. Does this endurance leader thing pass muster with regular leaders?

Let's look at Kalisha, a leader I consider an endurance leader in the making. She had remarkable success early in her career as a strategist at some of the most prestigious universities in the world. In her late thirties, Kalisha sought coaching after taking on a new position with significant operational and financial oversight and managing a 400-person team.

Moreover, she had returned to work after parental leave—another novel experience and form of adjustment.

Aware of her natural propensity to "sprint in everything I do,"[9] Kalisha's coaching goal was to build an approach to leadership that would not constantly deplete her energy and resources. She left her last job feeling drained and discouraged. She wanted to cultivate a connection to her new job, new team, and family that would keep her motivated and energized through the inevitable challenges while still maintaining her passion for the work she cared about deeply.

The first thing Kalisha and I worked on was understanding her ultimate mission. What is it that she wants to be known for thirty years from now? What would she want her child to be saying about her toward the end of her career? Kalisha recognized that her two main goals—having a successful professional career and being a great mother to her children—could coexist (previously, she felt like she had to choose one or the other). Furthermore, she recognized that part of her professional success needed to incorporate something intrinsically tied to her happiness—dance—whether in physical form or metaphor.

Acknowledging the importance of these two realities helped Kalisha make different choices as she began her new role: She set clear boundaries regarding working hours and expectations with herself, her boss, and her team. She opted to be more transparent with her team about her life priorities than in the past, which helped her live more authentically at work (something she strived to improve). It also provided her with a human connection with colleagues she hadn't previously appreciated or leveraged.

To ensure she was executing successfully upon her ultimate mission, Kalisha targeted small, incremental behaviors that could enhance her success as a leader and remain engaged with what mattered most to her. This kind of minimum viable effort (MVE) is the smallest unit of effort Kalisha could make to create sustainable change. (Stanford Researcher BJ Fogg first introduced this concept and later referenced it in his book *Tiny*

Habits;[10] it is also referenced in James Clear's book *Atomic Habits*.[11]) Kalisha selected small behaviors to set the tone she intended in her leadership; for example, she began incorporating dance metaphors into her work lexicon. As she did, she noticed her colleagues taking notice and paying more attention to her contributions. In her effort to be more authentic, she was becoming more influential.

Another focus for Kalisha has been getting the proper support straightaway. As she approached her new position, she recognized she could not achieve her long-term goals (developing a more accessible and practical leadership style while remaining strategic and visionary) without the proper coaching and guidance. As a result, she reached out for coaching well before starting her new role. By having a coach help her remain accountable before she even began in the new role, Kalisha hit the ground running and avoided the leadership habits that had previously interfered with her long-term success.

Kalisha's story isn't finished—far from it. Her long-term goals—building a legacy in her work and at home—are still decades in the making. But by starting her endurance leadership work now, she is choosing her leadership style with intention, focus, and the right priorities to keep her energized as she moves forward. Like all of us, she will face struggles and challenges. But by using excellent support, she can keep herself accountable, remain agile and adaptive, and execute in a disciplined and focused manner.

The Endurance Leader Model

The Endurance Leader Model (Figure 2) captures the foundational elements that endurance athletes and long-term leaders share. It establishes what is at the heart of delivering greatness in the long term.

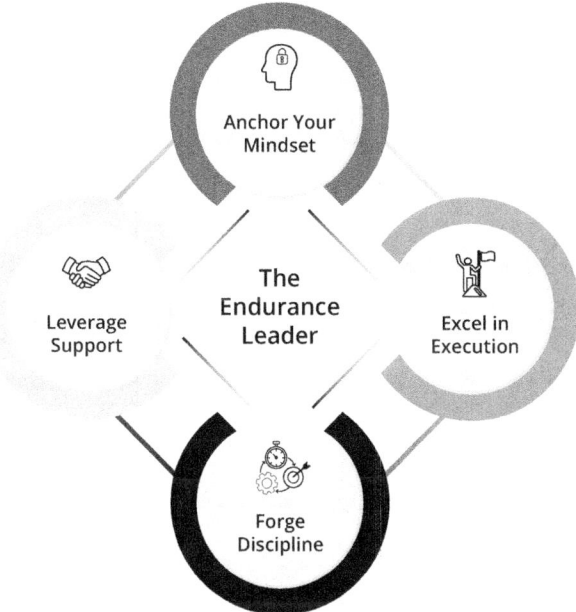

Figure 2: Endurance Leader Model

Within each quadrant are 4-5 core principles. The language comes from athletics, but as you will see, each element applies equally to the endurance leader.

To give you a flavor for the model's elements, you might enjoy seeing how they apply to some people you just met (see Figures 3, 4, and 5).

Figure 3. Endurance Leader Model application – Scott Rigsby

Scott Rigsby

Endurance Leader Quadrant	Commitment/ Behavior	Manifestation
Anchor Your Mindset	Driven by renewed energy and self-awareness, he vowed to reclaim his life and health.	In 2007, he became the first double amputee to complete the Ironman World Championship in Kona, Hawaii.
Excel in Execution	Commitment to training for over a year to complete the race.	A stringent training schedule and proclamations to friends and media held him accountable.
Forge Discipline	Dealt with the inevitable setbacks that occur during training and the race itself.	Finished the race despite agonizing pain and exhaustion.
Leverage Support	Leveraged a coach throughout. Trained for a purpose, specifically, supporting his charity.	Constantly used feedback to improve his timing, inform him of his liabilities, and adjust. Supporting others made the goals bigger than himself.

Figure 4. Endurance Leader Model application – Jimmy

Jimmy

Endurance Leader Quadrant	Commitment/ Behavior	Manifestation
Anchor Your Mindset	Motivated by his commitment to service, he vowed to leverage his skills and abilities to lead others.	Positive results for the hospital (best in class) within two years.
Excel in Execution	Countered work stress with running, rest, meditation, and daily use of the action-reflection cycle.	Set and achieved challenging but achievable milestones for building the hospital. Made progress every day. Committed to not working twelve- to fourteen-hour days.
Forge Discipline	Lessons from early life and endurance sports: "You make a commitment; you stick with it."	Worked through the obstacles and hard times to build a world-class facility. Dug deeper into his ultimate mission to stay focused and on course. Pivoted when needed.
Leverage Support	Used a myriad of leadership coaches, mentors, and his spouse as coaches and support.	Maintained perspective and focus throughout the hospital-building process. Remained focused on the bigger picture of life and personal priorities.

Figure 5. Endurance Leader Model application – Kalisha

Kalisha

Endurance Leader Quadrant	Commitment/ Behavior	Manifestation
Anchor Your Mindset	Aspiring to build a life and career that will make her child proud, she is committed to leading by enabling others.	Using a life passion (dance) as a metaphor, she is shifting dynamics within her team to build greater interdependence.
Excel in Execution	As a doer, she is challenging herself to set aside time to think and reflect.	Making incremental progress toward goals with realistic timelines. Using MVE, creating better balance, ensuring focused delivery as well as proper recovery.
Forge Discipline	Articulating new goals to others to stay accountable and stepping out of her comfort zone to try new leadership techniques.	Building agility in her leadership and getting recognized for a more authentic leadership style. Creating more spaces to try her new approach so she is not reliant on a single condition or instance to practice.
Leverage Support	Using a leadership coach. Requesting input from colleagues to help her calibrate progress.	Finding more gratitude and joy in her work. Feeling more internally congruent and eager to help others.

These leaders exemplify a common core: the discipline and character to push themselves for greatness—even when obstacles abound and the stakes are stacked against them—and the guts to thrive in adversity and move past quick wins to what truly matters.

Can You Be An Endurance Leader?

These stories may feel distant from your current challenges: You may be more worried about managing a hybrid team, the emerging role of artificial intelligence in work, or keeping your staff motivated when changes are constant and unpredictable. You may think the endurance leader model suits athletic-minded people, but not you. But the truth is, you *can* benefit from this model by asking yourself some critical questions, putting strategies into action, and holding yourself accountable. It can help you achieve your goals, but as the old saying goes, "It only works if you do!"

I invite you to reflect upon the Coach's Questions and make specific commitments in the Training Plan. Remember what I said in the preface: This is meant to be a workbook, so I encourage you to write in it, highlight it, or tear out pages and put them in your journal—whatever helps you get closer to being the leader you were meant to be.

Coach's Questions ▬ ▬ ▬ ▬ ▬ ▬ ▬ ▬ ▬

- How long do you want to be leading: Five years? Ten? Thirty? How clear is your plan for creating successful leadership over that time horizon?

- How are you currently managing your stressors? How effective are your strategies? If we asked your spouse/family/friends, what would they say?

- Where do you see yourself as strongest in the four parts of The Endurance Leader model? Where are you weakest?

- What do you want to achieve by reading this book? Where could you apply the principle of MVE to help you get closer to your goal?

Training Plan

- Set aside weekly dedicated time to focus on your long-term leadership development. Be specific and discrete about that time and determine how you will hold yourself accountable.
- Articulate the resources you will need on the journey to your destination: physical, emotional, tactical, and supportive. Who and what will you need to support you and keep you focused and energized for this work?
- What keeps you tough during the most challenging moments? Write that down and keep it handy, as you will need it throughout this journey.

Lao Tzu famously said, "The journey of a thousand miles begins with a single step." Are you ready to take the first step to becoming an endurance leader?

PART II

Anchor Your Mindset

Chapter 2

Discern Your Mission

*If you don't make the time to work on creating the life
that you want, you're going to spend a lot of time
dealing with a life you don't want.*
KEVIN NGO

A Mission-Inspired Journey

In 2007, I began competing in triathlons to raise money for blood cancer research through an organization called Team in Training. This combination met some of my deepest needs: to serve others in a way that encouraged me to remain healthy. When I decided to compete in an Ironman race, I aimed to raise money for another nonprofit, the Washington, DC, chapter of Back on My Feet (BoMF). BoMF's mission is to "empower people to overcome the cycles of poverty, homelessness, or addiction through the power of fitness, community & employment resources."[12]

In the week leading up to the race, the director of the BoMF DC chapter sent me an astounding email: 141 messages addressed to me with words of encouragement, cheers, and prayers from around the country—one for every mile of the 140.6 miles of swimming, biking, and running. The statements written by staff and BoMF members (people transitioning from homelessness into secure jobs and housing) were breathtaking, humbling, and moving. These people, who had struggled with so much adversity, were encouraging *me*. Throughout the race, I pulled the list out and read the words several times. Its ability to buoy me was profound, and from those words, I gained the strength I needed to finish the race.

These messages were powerful because they went beyond kindness, praise, and encouragement. They spoke to the heart of my ultimate mission: love, leadership, and service. When I faced tremendous adversity and self-doubt on the race course, their encouragement reflected my beliefs about what is most important, what grounds me, and what drives me. Digging deep to remember my mission helped me cross that Ironman finish line.

The Definition Of Mission

Johnson & Johnson's Human Performance Institute provides a resource for people to determine how to live according to their purpose.[13] I call this the ultimate mission. Without it, leaders can become lost and overwhelmed by life's storms and stressors. How many leaders have you seen who seem beleaguered, tired, and unmotivated by the middle of their careers?

Evidence exists that midlife crises are often crises of mission.[14] When leaders leave a job they dislike, it is often because they have little connection with their work on a personal level – in other words, they cannot see the relationship between their work and their ultimate mission.

The ultimate mission is essential in creating a connection with everyday work, but it can also play a critical role in buoying you as a leader when times get tough. For example, it may be hard to stay focused or motivated if you are going through an organizational restructuring and related layoffs. But if you know what it is that grounds you, the reason in your soul why you are in your job, and what positive impact you are having, you are much more likely to remain steady, focused, and see your way to the end with strength and compassion.

One's ultimate mission is built on higher-order drivers and motivators: A faith or belief system, a commitment to the common good, or a desire for broad social impact, for example. To determine their ultimate mission, endurance leaders ask themselves:

- What am I uniquely on the planet to do?
- What do I want people to say about me at the end of my career? At the end of my life?
- What makes my life worth living?
- What is my headstone mission (i.e., if I wrote out what I wanted my gravestone marker to say, what would it be?)

By answering these existential questions, we can clearly understand our identity, what matters to us, and what we want to do with "our one wild and precious life," in the immortal words of poet Mary Oliver.[15]

Ultimate Mission Examples

A few examples of individuals who reflect their mission may help this feel more actionable and less lofty. Let's first look at endurance leader Thasunda Brown Duckett, CEO of TIAA. She describes her mission through her experience of growing up with little financial stability. She states that her mission is to "make sure my parents and people like my parents are making the best financial decisions they can."[16] For Duckett, her life goal is to have a lasting impact on entire groups of people by helping them be financially successful. She can reflect on this truth when times get tough to keep her motivated and energized.

In 2019, aspiring endurance athlete Chris Nikic told his dad he wanted to complete an Ironman race. Taking on a race of this magnitude is hard for anyone, but for Nikic, who has Down syndrome, this was an astounding and potentially impossible declaration. Nikic had never completed a triathlon; in fact, no person with Down syndrome had ever completed an Ironman race.

Many would have discouraged Nikic, trying to gently sway him away from what they would have seen as a fruitless pursuit. However, Chris and his father believed it might be possible if they made a realistic plan and trained smartly and consistently. In 2020, at age twenty-one, Nikic achieved his goal of becoming the first known person with Down syndrome to finish an Ironman race. Chris's mission is to be 1 percent better in one aspect of his life daily,[17] and nowhere was that more evident than completing this race.

Challenge And Opportunity

Many athletes and leaders tend to avoid or overlook the work of their ultimate mission. Why? It is easier and perhaps more familiar to focus on the quick wins. For example, in athletics, someone might get motivated to join a gym for the low cost of joining or sign up for a local 5k running race, so they complete it with their friends and get a cool finisher medal.

But what happens when the event is over, or the gym membership is now just a gym membership? Many people fall off the exercise wagon because the short-term win has lost its luster, and the inner motivation to continue day after day is just not there. They return to a state of nonengagement in athletics, as evidenced by the fact that most of the population engages in less than the recommended 120 minutes of exercise per week.[18]

However, those who translate their short-term efforts into regular practice have found internal motivation to continue. Deci and Ryan (2000) showed that people often start exercising because of a high perceived value or high personal importance; however, they stick with exercise when they find it pleasurable, fun, and satisfying.[19] When people can see their mission (= high personal importance) resulting in *satisfaction*, they are deeply internally motivated.

On the competition field or in the boardroom, why aren't more people engaged in understanding their ultimate mission? The adage says, "If it were easy, everybody would do it." A few things might get in our way:

- *Inertia is incongruous with deep reflection.* We avoid deep self-reflection because it tends to make us uncomfortable. It calls us to consider mortality, spirituality, life decisions, and self-perception. Moreover, it might make us feel like we need to change something. It's easier to stay in our comfort zones, even if they are unsatisfying, because we are used to the routine.

- *It takes time.* Trying to understand your ultimate mission does not consist of simply articulating a catchphrase or listing out your goals. It might take years of analyzing your motivators, looking at your life, and thinking about what you believe, value, and cherish. With time as our least available asset, making the time for such a luxury might feel impossible. You might think, "I barely get time in for a decent dinner; now I need to transform myself?" We are unwilling to slow down long enough to consider its importance to our life satisfaction.

- *It will change you.* When I first articulated my ultimate mission, I came to the startling realization that I had to quit my highly lucrative job. It was inconsistent with my drives, values, and motivators. That's scary stuff. If you are unwilling to be changed, you may need to do more work to be ready for this journey.

- *You fall short every single day.* Pursuing the ultimate mission is a lifelong journey. If you seek it, you will fall short of your goal every day – even if you've made significant progress. It's much easier to focus on small wins and not consider the bigger picture.

Let me present some reasons why you might want to work on your ultimate mission:

- *It's calling you anyway.* I've yet to meet someone who didn't think they had a higher purpose. Whether spiritual, family, community, civic, or personal, most people believe there is more to life than just what we are experiencing today. Ignoring the call of that purpose is like trying not to see the sunshine—it will be there every day, whether you care to acknowledge it or not.

- *It creates deep motivation.* What truly drives you? Is it to receive your paycheck or get a new title? I'd argue those are more means to an end than true motivators in and of themselves. In other words, while external factors may incentivize you, it's more likely that what drives you and motivates you are internal motivators, like living your purpose, having great relationships, or having a meaningful impact on your community. A study by Çınar et al.[20] showed that while extrinsic and intrinsic factors affected employees completing tasks, intrinsic factors were found to be more motivating than extrinsic factors. So, while title, prestige, and wealth may motivate leaders, they may ultimately be less motivating than those leaders' internal drivers.

- *It will keep you focused on what truly matters to you.* Once you have defined your ultimate mission, it becomes like a North Star: you tend to see it wherever you go. It guides you, keeping you aligned with what is ultimately most important.

Remember Preethi's statement from earlier, "I don't know how much longer I can do this?" I asked her, "Preethi, what do you want to be known for toward the end of your life?" She looked at me quizzically, then sat back thoughtfully with a huge sigh. After a quiet moment, she said with no shortage of emotion in her voice, "I want to be known as a loving wife, a great mom, and a great example for my children. I want them to see I was passionate about my work and made a difference as a woman in leadership. Those will be the most important descriptors anyone could use for me." This, I declared, was her ultimate mission.

After we sat in that space for a few moments, I asked her what in her current work reflected those things. Her first reaction was to laugh and say, "Absolutely nothing!" But then she recognized some specific places where this future state was manifesting in her work: she had increased the number of women in her division, a part of the company that was traditionally light on female representation. She was also proud that she had helped structure and support several affinity groups, including groups for women of color and those committed to LGBTQIA+ equality.

As she talked, some of the classic Preethi returned to the conversation: she spoke animatedly and enthusiastically about the work done in those spaces. With some further guidance, she began linking these successes to her ultimate mission, recognizing that her children would be proud of her impact as a female leader. The remainder of our session focused on creating daily reflection opportunities to link successes in her leadership back to the intrinsic motivator of being a female leader of whom her children will be proud. By the end of our session, she had so much more energy she practically bounced out of her chair.

If Preethi can do it, you can too. I will help you get started.

Coach's Questions ▰ ▰ ▰ ▰ ▰ ▰ ▰ ▱ ▱ ▱

- What are you uniquely on this planet to do?

- How will your ultimate mission bring you greater satisfaction?

- If I followed you for one month, would I know your mission by observing you? What evidence would I see?

- What are you committed to changing to live closer to your mission?

Training Plan

- *Articulate your life's ultimate mission.* Can you verbalize your ultimate mission? If not, devote some time to figuring it out. If you knew you would die tomorrow, would you be proud of how close you came? Take heed: this is a spiritually and emotionally consuming activity.

- *Impact of mission.* If you were living even 10 percent closer to your mission, how would it impact your:
  - Work
  - Family
  - Health
  - Perspective
  - Community

- *Articulate the "obstacle" story.* Determine what story you might be telling yourself about why you can't live closer to your mission.

- *Write a new story.* Rewrite the story that allows you to live closer to your mission.

- *Bring your mission story alive.* Find time daily to reflect on your successes and connect them to your mission.

Chapter 3

Establish Your Baseline

Start where you are. Use what you have. Do what you can.
ARTHUR ASHE

Now that we have our ultimate mission, how can we get closer to achieving it? As in business and athletics, it starts with knowing how close we are to the goal. The best way to get to where we want to be is to know where we are, which requires getting some baseline data.

The Criticality Of A Good Baseline

For Chris Nikic to complete the Ironman race, he and his dad Nik spent considerable time up front appraising where Chris was physically and where he needed to be to finish the race successfully. Could Chris learn to cover the 2.4-mile swim when he had little swimming experience? Could he manage the 112 miles of cycling without losing focus or falling off the bike? Could he make the time cutoff? What about the twenty-six-mile run?

By starting with baseline fitness testing, they evaluated how much training Chris would need to become physically strong enough to complete each leg of the race. Less known was how Chris's mental capabilities would fare during the training. Could he cognitively grasp the subtle factors involved in each sport and the race itself? Could he keep the mental order needed to transition successfully between each race segment?

Over the next eighteen months, Chris and Nik developed a training plan to build Chris' physical fitness. In addition to increasing his capabilities in each triathlon discipline, they also worked on muscle strength and conditioning. As they continually met the training plan goals, Nik also saw his son's cognitive capacities expand: "His memory improved, his social skills, and everyday tasks that he used to have problems with became much easier for him. His confidence has gone up, too. The impact has been incredible."[21]

Chris and Nik did not try to get Chris ready for the soonest possible Ironman. They intentionally picked a race over a year away, knowing how much training it would take for Chris to be prepared for such an endeavor. By conducting a realistic appraisal of the gap between where Chris was and where he needed to be, they built a realistic and meaningful plan to achieve his goal *and* to live Chris's 1 percent better mission.

Establishing An Endurance Leader Baseline

Business leaders are experts at baseline data. To meet long-term strategic goals, they must regularly evaluate their current starting point; otherwise, they might push too hard, not move fast enough, misallocate resources, take too many or too few risks, or any other of several missteps because they haven't understood the difference between where they are and where they need to be. If the goal is to grow revenue by 400 percent in the next five years, *how* the organization does this will depend on current revenue trends, market positioning, economic factors, internal capabilities, and more.

By understanding their baseline leadership behavior, endurance leaders can determine the best strategies to get closer to their ultimate mission. Knowing their leadership strengths and gaps can be critical to effective execution.

When I began working with Peggy, we discussed the best ways to understand her impact on her team and the organization. Peggy's ultimate mission is to advocate for, serve, and support others in all aspects of her life. She knew she had work areas, but she also felt sure there were blind spots that might be keeping her from being fully aware of where and how she should focus her leadership energy (and how she could get closer to her ultimate mission).

To help Peggy establish her baseline, we conducted a personality-based assessment that helped her understand some of her personality qualities and how they could manifest at work. Next, I collected stakeholder feedback that helped Peggy see her strengths and development areas and identify her blind spots (evident from differences between her self-view and others' views of her behavior). Furthermore, through quantitative measures, we could see the degree of difference between Peggy's view and others' view. This helped us create a realistic coaching action plan, as we knew that bigger gaps would mean more effort. Like Chris and Nik Nikic, our baseline data helped us drive toward meaningful and achievable behaviors to increase success.

Baseline Tools

As a consultant and coach, I use several tools to help leaders understand their baseline behavior. Here are a few:

- *Personality assessment.* Personality data is relatively fixed, so we don't expect to reassess it later and get different results. However, it does provide a type of baseline information about the individual. When we think about leadership, remember from Figure 1 that our first focus is on leading ourselves. Personality data helps us understand this baseline and how it can affect our behavior. This can be beneficial information for focused development and coaching.
- *360-degree assessments/stakeholder feedback.* One of the most effective ways to establish baseline data about our leadership strengths and gaps is to ask the people we lead and work with. After all, aren't they the best ones to help us understand the impact of our leadership

behavior? A 360-degree feedback assessment is so-called because it provides leaders with behavioral data from themselves, their boss, peers, direct reports, and customers or other relevant stakeholders (see Figure 6). It is an excellent tool for gaining insight into how others perceive the leader and how those views compare with the leader's self-view.

Figure 6. 360-Degree Feedback Review Process[22]

360-Degree Feedback

A 360-degree process is often automated (and increasingly AI-enabled) but substituting or supplementing that data with stakeholder interviews can be an excellent way to gain greater insight into the leader's behavior.

- *Observation.* Another good way to obtain baseline data is to be observed by others. When I begin coaching engagements with my clients, I try to observe them in their day-to-day environment: sometimes, I follow them around like a puppy for a day; other times, I join them for critical meetings (live or virtual), where I quietly collect data on how they are showing up. By watching how my coaching client behaves, I can help her target specific behavior changes in critical areas.

The Johari Window

One of the wonderful things about baseline data is it can identify blind spots. We all have them; what is essential for the endurance leader is to make them as small as possible. The Johari Window[23] (see Figure 7) is a great model for leaders as they attempt to understand their style and how it is understood by others. The model shows that we are all aware of certain qualities about ourselves and clueless about others. Let's look at the meaning of each quadrant:

Figure 7. The Johari Window

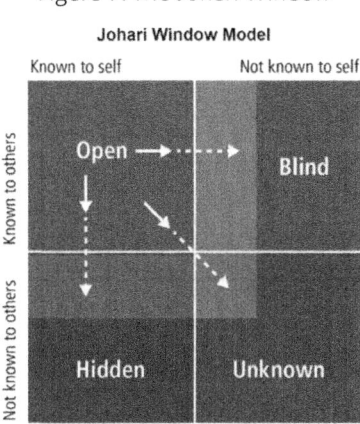

- *Unknown.* These are things about us that neither we nor others know. For example, you may have a great singing voice, but if you never tried to sing, you may not know that—nor would others. Or a cyclist competing in the Tour de France might be a very gifted runner, but if all they've ever done is cycle, they wouldn't know about their running abilities.
- *Open.* There are things about us that we know and others know, too. We understand those to be open and available qualities. For example, you might be a good listener. You know this because others have complimented you for your listening skills, and when you think about the behaviors that demonstrate good listening, you know they describe you. This is often the case for elite athletes as well. Our Tour de France athlete knows about their cycling abilities and is considered by others to be among the best in the world.
- *Hidden.* We all have qualities we know and keep hidden from others (or at least we try). For example, you might get anxious before you

present in public. But when people see you speak in public, they see someone who is calm, poised, and confident. You've hidden that nervous part so that others won't experience it. Returning to our Tour cyclist, this person might naturally have a vision issue, but surgical interventions and coping techniques have made it a nonissue when they ride and compete.

- *Blind.* These are qualities about us that others know, but we don't. Reducing our blind spots comes from a willingness to learn about ourselves. That might be through someone teaching you something you didn't know before. Or it might be through gathering information from others about our behavior. This is a challenging thing to do. As humans, we all have difficulty acknowledging and accepting our weaknesses. As one of my psychology grad school professors used to say, "We are all the protagonists of our own story." For a leader like Peggy, this is precisely what she was hoping for in our baseline activities: the opportunity to gain new insights into where she falls short in her leadership of the organization and her team. For our Tour de France cyclist, this might be recognizing that he spends too much time looking behind him during races, which not only affects his aerodynamics but also seems to demotivate him and reduce his pedaling speed.

The Johari window is beneficial when leaders want to move from good to exceptional. When we are already good at something, it can be hard to see slight differences that can move us from great to greater. Like a blind spot in your car, something just out of view can create disastrous effects if you don't know it's there.

It might be that your blind spot is the overuse of one of your strengths. For example, you may be gifted at synthesizing and simplifying ideas in meetings to create clarity and a path forward. However, if you overuse this strength, you might prematurely cut off idea generation or prevent others from summarizing ideas and articulating the path forward. No one wants you to stop using your strength, but to walk that careful balance between helpful and excessive.

The Importance Of Self-Awareness

Juan-Carlos (JC) and I sat staring at each other in a helpless impasse. JC's organization had hired me to assess candidates for a vacant director role. JC, a senior manager, had applied for this promotion-level position. I interviewed him and the other candidates and authored reports about their fit for the role, which was one factor in the hiring decision. JC ultimately was not selected.

The report highlighted that JC is smart, ambitious, and good at driving results but lacks self-awareness. JC and I reviewed the report's results to help him understand his strengths and gap areas relative to the role. True to form, JC welcomed and highlighted feedback about his strengths but defended against and downplayed his gaps. His lack of self-awareness was on full display, creating this impasse. Without self-awareness, there is no baseline, knowledge of gaps, or motivation for change. Without motivation for change, I am useless as a coach, and the leader is powerless to improve.

Awareness of how people experience us is critical in reaching a desired level of leadership influence. In 2010, JP Flaum and others at Green Peak Partners worked with Cornell University to study the factors that most predict executive success. Their study found that self-awareness is most significantly correlated with executive success.[24] Unfortunately, JC was unwilling to embrace these truths. He may struggle to achieve his desired career progression, which he hopes will lead to an executive-level role.

Let's contrast JC's attitude regarding change with Alex's. As vice president of a large construction company, Alex has delivered outstanding results by taking on several challenging assignments and managing complex projects in multiple geographies. Executive leadership sees Alex's potential for higher levels of leadership. In our first coaching conversation, Alex mentioned how their career had flourished at the company. However, they also recognized that what they had been doing to be successful thus far would not get them to higher levels of leadership.

Still in their thirties, Alex sees a long and fruitful leadership career at the company but says, "If I don't grow and change, I might be a good manager, but I'll never be a great leader." While Alex had some ideas about where they needed to improve as a leader, they also recognized that they might have blind spots that could affect their ability to be successful. Alex's motivation to identify the baseline between where they are as a leader and where they want to be helped Alex clarify their goals.

For example, while they knew that patience was an issue, Alex didn't know (until we completed stakeholder interviews) that this was mostly an issue with direct reports. That information helped Alex narrow their goal from "exhibiting more patience" to "being more coach-like with my team members in all interactions."

Coaching with Alex has been a joy. As measured in my follow-up conversations with stakeholders, Alex logged consistent improvements with team members within a month of receiving stakeholder feedback. Even more exciting, Alex's exhibition of more coach-like behaviors has provided more visibility to the team members, resulting in some being promoted. Alex is less irritable, more consistent, and more energized for broader leadership.

Athletes and leaders who establish their baseline get impressive results (and are closer to their mission) because they know their starting position. Consider some strategies for establishing your baseline so you, too, can understand what will be necessary to achieve your goal.

Coach's Questions ▬ ▬ ▬ ▬ ▬ ▬ ▬ ▒ ▒ ▒

- What leadership behaviors are you currently demonstrating that reflect your ultimate mission? Are there missed opportunities or gaps? Adroitly appraising these will help you establish a baseline toward meaningful growth.

- How willing are you to uncover blind spots? What could you do to expose them?

- How can you keep your self-awareness high? Who can help you?

Training Plan

- Articulate your mission and baseline to understand the gaps:
  - My ultimate mission is _____. For example, this paraphrases one client's mission: "My ultimate mission is to make a direct and meaningful difference in the lives of as many professional women from underrepresented groups as possible."
  - My baseline toward my ultimate mission is _____. Continuing the example above, "My baseline is I'm currently indirectly impacting women through my corporate work. I am building the financial foundation needed for the

investment group I want to establish to support these women. But I don't have the investor backing to launch a startup investment fund, and I haven't built enough traction with my target market yet."

- o You might also refer to the Training Plan in Chapter 2. Are there additional insights that would inform your baseline?

- Use the Johari Window and list your open strengths and development areas. What hidden or undervalued qualities/strengths might help you reach your goals? How can you reduce your blind spots? The client's example continues:
  - o Strengths: "I'm a proven CEO with a strong record of helping others grow and develop. I know how to build profitability inside an organization and build personal wealth. I can help others learn those skills."

  - o Underleveraged strength: "I am a good public speaker and can influence well. But I hide behind my introversion and discomfort and don't do it enough."

  - o Development areas: "I am a risk taker, which can be a strength and a liability. I can be impatient and lose interest in things quickly. I also haven't been as visible to the community I want to serve."

  - o Increasing knowledge: "I will survey my team members and community network for more information about where I can improve and use that data to help me build a more precise baseline. This way, I can set the right goals to make this mission a reality."

- Plan to keep your self-awareness high. Create a cadence for feedback from trusted peers and your boss. When you get defensive, ask yourself, "What part of this is true? How can I learn from that truth to grow?"

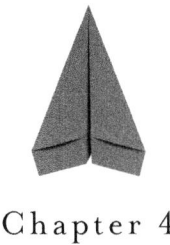

Chapter 4

Build Your Training Plan

A goal without a plan is just a wish.
ANTOINE DE SAINT-EXUPÉRY

Now that you understand your relationship to your ultimate mission, it is essential to develop a training plan. But before we start discussing plans, we need to consider—and potentially challenge—how we understand goals.

Rethinking Goal Setting

You probably wouldn't be reading this book if you hadn't already been successful in goal setting throughout life. But your ultimate mission is more of an ideal than a singular goal. So, how do you plan for an ideal? This is a much more complex task that many leaders do not have the language or experience to create.

In striving to achieve our mission, reframing how we think about goals can be helpful. In his book *Atomic Habits*, James Clear discusses the importance of inverting the model that most of us have around goals.[25] Typically, we see goals in terms of outcomes; then, we try to build habits that will result in that outcome and assume that our identity will develop because of those habits. According to Clear, our thinking looks something like this:

Outcome ⇨ Habit ⇨ Identity

Examples are, "I want to earn 20 percent more this year," or "I want to lose thirty pounds," or "I want to finish a marathon." Then, we try to build habits around those outcomes and expect the habits to say something significant about us: "She's so talented and special; she's making so much money." Or "He is so strong and fit; he lost all that weight!" Or "She finished a marathon; she is such an athlete."

Clear contends that this sets us up for failure. If we fail to establish the habits, we fail at creating that identity. So, for example, if you are like most humans who lose weight and fail to keep it off, you may feel like a failure or doomed to be an unfit and weak person (identity). Talk about interfering with intrinsic motivation!

Instead, Clear suggests we reverse the order:

Identity ⇨ Habit ⇨ Outcome

Starting with identity, we focus on who we are rather than what we do. For example, "I want to be a healthy person." What do healthy people do? They build healthy eating habits, don't overdo food or drink, and exercise regularly. The outcome? Often weight loss, but also lower body fat, better sleep and more energy.

First, Begin With Identity

The outcome-identity problem is often evident in neophyte endurance athletes: they usually choose a race they want to finish (outcome) and then build their habits around it. Like our weight loss example, the problem is that if something interferes with those habits (e.g., an injury or illness), the athlete can feel like a failure.

Seasoned endurance athletes instead adopt the identity of an athlete. Even when not racing (for an outcome), they maintain their mental and physical discipline through exercise, diet, massage, and sleep. If their training schedule is interrupted, they simply continue their other endurance athlete habits. Their identity is in who they are, not what they do.

Endurance leaders strive to link their identity to their ultimate mission. As a result, selecting goals that reflect their identity is much more likely to be intrinsically motivating. If you choose outcome-based goals, such as, "I want to be seen as a better listener" or "I want to change the boss's perception of me," your leadership identity will be tied to those outcomes.

A prime example comes from Peggy, whom you met earlier. A strong and talented senior leader, she spent her career building her way up in the organization. She was known for her approachable but no-nonsense style, care for her people, and fierce commitment to results. When we started coaching work together, Peggy struggled with a vicious cycle of emotional ups and downs based mainly on her perception of her leadership performance. She had a noble outcome goal of micromanaging less. The problem was she rarely observed when she was successful at this and mostly noticed when she wasn't. This created occasional highs but a lot of emotional lows for her. At those moments, she would say, "I'm a total failure." (Can you hear the identity element in there? Not "I failed at x," but "I *am* a failure"). Those lows would negatively affect how Peggy's team experienced her, exacerbating the situation.

After articulating her ultimate mission (advocating, serving, and supporting others in all aspects of her life), Peggy built her leadership identity around it. Instead of defining her leadership success through her success at not micromanaging (outcome), her identity was focused on acting like a patient and poised leader (identity) focused on serving her team. She defined behaviors that were consistent with those qualities.

When she inevitably fell into micromanagement, she used cognitive reframing to say, "OK, that doesn't reflect my desired identity and mission of serving my team. What could I do to serve my team better next time?" The sting of behavioral failure was removed because identity has much more flexibility, nuance, and options than a specific outcome. Over time, Peggy grew in strategic engagement with her team and felt she was more closely living her mission. More importantly, she was more forgiving of herself and more emotionally consistent. This is the way endurance leaders set and achieve goals.

Second, Build Your Plan

Let's assume you've made some progress on rooting your goals in your identity. How can we set up a training plan that will reflect that identity and get you closer to your ultimate mission?

As with all long-term goals, endurance athletes translate those into more manageable chunks. A long-distance cyclist may train for nearly a year for a 2000k cycling journey. She must break her training into shorter goals to be ready for that trip. She will likely have her entire training plan mapped out in advance, with periodic goals, such as monthly, weekly, and daily training targets. Looking at a single day, the training may not look like much, but each goal builds upon the last one. Slowly, she gets stronger and more capable of longer distances.

How does an endurance leader develop a plan for their ultimate mission? You may recall that Kalisha's ultimate mission focused on having a robust professional career and being a great mother to her children. Part of her professional aspiration was to be in high enough positions to advocate for more professional women, particularly women of color. Kalisha identified that obtaining a C-suite role would help her be in that position.

Kalisha is two roles away from that level, so she thinks it will take five to six years to get there. A closer goal is a senior vice president role (the level between her and the C-suite), which might be two to three years away. With these realistic baseline appraisals in mind, we could more meaningfully segment her goals. For each goal, we identified key performance indicators (KPIs) that, if achieved, would demonstrate her readiness for the next goal/role.

Based on her goals for the next eighteen months, we translated a few goals into specific weekly and daily targets. For example, we determined that prioritization was something she could train every day through a daily review of priorities and a weekly check-in with her boss and her team on those goals (see Figure 8).

Figure 8. Kalisha's Training Plan (partial)

	Goal	When achieved	KPIs
Ultimate Mission	To be a great wife, mother, and leader	• Never finished • Lifelong work	• Feedback from family • Impact on professional women of color
Long-term goal	C-Suite role	5-6 years	• Leading organizational vision • Demonstrated differentiated strategic leadership • Leading through complexity • Building organizational capacity • Modeling inclusive and people-centered leadership others want to follow
Short-term goal	SVP role	2-3 years	• Build a high-performing Division that reflects inclusion • Lead strategy and vision efforts for new technologies • Demonstrate clear links between business performance and inclusion practices
2-year goal	Meet some of SVP role goals	18-36 months	• TBD based on year one success

1-year goal	Meet some of SVP role goals	1-18 months	• Develop a division-wide hiring strategy and develop metrics that link ROI with inclusionary hiring practices • Lead technology sourcing strategy team, produce a differentiated strategy to the Executive Committee • Build stronger critical prioritization skills in the face of accelerated timeframes and complexity

Following a relatively straightforward mapping technique, we translated what seemed to Kalisha like a squishy ultimate mission into something she could start executing daily. She now had a training plan.

A few key concepts, influenced heavily by endurance athlete language, can help build a successful training plan:

- *Calibrate your goals.* Building a training plan that connected Kalisha to her ultimate mission helped her build intrinsic motivation, organize her efforts, and provide direction. But she knew that changing demands and daily pressures could pull her into short-term sprint mode and forget her plan. To help her, she shared her training plan with her boss, a few close colleagues, her mentor (an SVP), and her family. They ensured that the goals she selected were aligned with her ultimate mission and her periodic steps along the way.

- *Track your progress.* Part of what motivated Kalisha was tracking her progress against her daily goals. We used a green/yellow/red system on her daily progress-tracking sheet (coded in shades of gray here, see Figure 9). If she used the prioritization system that day, she color-coded it green. If she did it partially, she coded it yellow. If she didn't do it at all, she coded it red. Being internally competitive, this system resonated with Kalisha. She found herself pushing for weeks of all-greens. She was particularly motivated when she could code green on the weekly check-ins with her boss and team and got feedback that the prioritization system was working.

Figure 9. Kalisha's progress tracking example

January		Prioritization used?	Green = Yes (Medium Gray)	Yellow = Partial (Light Gray)	Red = No (Dark Gray)	
0	MONDAY	TUESDAY	WEDNESDAY	THURSDAY	FRIDAY	SATURDAY
1	2 yes	3 yes	4 partial	5 yes	6 no	7 Team feedback: better focus and clarity this week but slow week
8	9 no	10 no	11 no	12 yes	13 yes	14 Team feedback: distractions created a rocky start, back on track but missed...
15	16 yes	17 partial	18 yes	19 yes	20 partial	21 Team feedback: better but need greater consistency at end of week
22	23 yes	24 yes	25 yes	26 yes	27 yes	28 Nailed it! Team feedback: great clarity in discussions and ...
29	30 yes	31 yes	1	2	3	4 Keeping up the momentum from last week...

- *Retest and adjust.* Athletes often devote time in their training to test against their baseline. This helps them know if they have made gains. Progress is usually small, but small gains are critical to sustainability when you complete an endurance race. In Kalisha's case, we didn't know if our selected goals would materialize into gains. So, we retested the plan every six weeks by reviewing all training plan behaviors with her boss (she also talked about her personal goals with her family). We looked to the boss for feedback about small gains and if he thought they would bring her closer to being SVP eligible. The size of the gain was less important than the fact that it was progress. Sometimes, the goals weren't materializing into the progress we wanted, or they didn't seem to link solidly to her SVP goals. We adjusted and reset the goals.

- *Use periodization techniques.* One concept often used in endurance athlete training plans is called periodization.[26] To explain in a simplified application to endurance athletes, by building specific periods of rest or reduced effort into their training calendars, athletes can achieve higher performance and reduce the risk of injury. In endurance leaders, this can also be true. After every six-week meeting with her boss, Kalisha and I determined that the next week would be less focused on her specific daily goals. She might focus instead on listening to a podcast about prioritization or have one of her team members lead the technology initiatives for the week. In other words, by giving her brain a chance to rest from (or modify) the daily focus on improvement, she could return the following week with renewed focus and energy.

As you build your training plan, recognize that it might not be clear initially. It's ok not to have a perfect plan; of course, plans can and often should change. But by building a plan, you are much more likely to get a step closer to what is most meaningful, impactful, and life-enriching for you.

Coach's Questions ▬ ▬ ▬ ▬ ▬ ▬ ▬ ▬ ▬

- Thinking about your existing goals, are you trying to change an outcome, or are you working toward an identity (a la James Clear)? How much would your relationship with your goals change if you flipped the order to identity first?

- If you don't develop a plan for achieving your ultimate mission, how will you achieve it? Are you expecting it to be something you will attend to later in life? Or that it will just happen with enough focus? What is possible if you make it part of your leadership goals now?

Training Plan

- Using Table 1 (the **Identity** ⇨ **Habit** ⇨ **Outcome** model), map out your responses:

  - What is my identity? (informed by your ultimate mission)

  - What are some of the habits that I want to engage in that reflect this identity?

  - If I have these habits, what will be the outcomes?

  - What goals will get me closer to my mission?

- Now begin to map the Goals from Table 1 to the specific training plan in Table 2 (focusing on work for the endurance leader):

  - Set work-related goals that will help you achieve the goals you set in Table 1.

  - Select realistic timeframes for the achievement of each goal.

  - Identify KPIs that will help you determine progress.

  - Determine how you will implement your training plan, when you will review it, how, and with whom.

Table 1. Identity First Goal Planning

Identity	Habit	Outcome	Goal

Table 2. Training Plan

	Goal	Achievement Date	KPIs
Ultimate Mission			
Long-term goal			
Short-term goal			
Two-year goal			
One-year goal			

Chapter 5

Anticipate And Plan
For Obstacles

Life is what happens while you're busy making other plans.
ALLEN SAUNDERS (NO, NOT JOHN LENNON)

A Shifting Identity

My client Darnell, a long-distance runner, was frustrated. For the past decade, Darnell has completed at least one marathon or ultramarathon every year, and he expected that this year would be no different. However, he had a happy problem: his startup business was growing quickly, and he hoped to double his revenue in the next twelve months.

As he and his team worked to prepare the organization for scaling up, Darnell found that he had less and less time to train. How could he keep his running training goal when time was becoming scarcer every day? His initial strategy, which is what many endurance athletes and leaders do, is to try to cram.

Here's an illustration: Darnell's typical goal was to run thirty to forty miles per week. He was now struggling to get even ten miles in during the work week, so he began trying to make up the rest on the weekend, often logging double-digit runs on Saturday and Sunday. This strategy had multiple deleterious effects: not only was he increasing his chance of injury, but he was also completely exhausted by Sunday evening, exactly when he needed to feel refreshed for a busy week ahead.

How could Darnell achieve his marathon goal and ensure the business could be successful? Well…he couldn't, at least without a whole bunch of risk. But that's not the end of the story.

Darnell and I looked hard at the marathon goal and what it meant for his identity. As we discussed previously, Darnell had built his identity as an athlete around the successful completion of a yearly marathon (outcome). We began working to shift his identity to that of an endurance athlete and an endurance leader. I challenged him to expand what it meant to be an endurance athlete.

He discovered that it meant leading a lifestyle of healthy and challenging activity for several decades, which didn't necessarily mean he had to do a marathon. He realized that shorter-distance races, such as half marathons, might allow him to maintain his health goals without the massive time commitment required for marathon training. Darnell committed to running a maximum of twenty miles per week, and while initially it was hard for him to do less, he began to enjoy it. He also started running more frequently with friends who could manage running with him at these new distances. This also helped him meet some social needs while achieving his health goals.

Because of his shifts in thinking, Darnell found more time for rest, strategic planning, forecasting, innovating, and listening to advisors, mentors, and his team—all things he needed to be doing to continue to grow his business. He seized some market opportunities and recognized (with some help) some holes in his organizational and operational structures that he was able to fix. He and his team celebrated doubling the company revenue one year later as planned.

It wasn't easy for Darnell to overcome the time obstacle. Shifting how he understood himself as an athlete meant changing an identity he had worked hard to build and maintain. But thinking of endurance as an identity instead of an outcome, he found fresh solutions and some grace for himself. Darnell fully expects to get back to marathoning someday, and because he has also done a better job delegating to his team, he could potentially have more time to devote to training. But he's decided to wait a bit longer until the business stabilizes.

Disruption Detection

Distractions and disruptions are a part of every business. Most businesses incorporate anticipated obstacles or disruptions into annual or quarterly business planning. Some are consistent and predictable, such as cyclical surges in business or fourth-quarter sales pressures. Some are unusual, but companies can see them developing from a distance, such as economic changes and recessionary conditions.

While the response to these conditions differs, business leaders find ways to think about their plans under each condition. They might implement a Plan B option or modify expectations to meet these new conditions. In either case, successful organizations recognize that achieving their long-term goals is bound to have disruptions. Rather than be surprised by them, they plan for them. As Yossi Sheffi's 2015 MIT Sloan article states, "…detecting the potential for a disruption to your business—ideally before that disruption occurs—can help you reduce its negative impact."[27]

Endurance leaders do the same. They recognize that their ultimate mission goals are long-term and not solely reliant on what gets done today, this week, or this year. Sometimes, meeting the goal means taking a side route or even backtracking on occasion. As one endurance leader, Murphy, told me, "You don't get to decide how big the wave is; you just have to ride it."[28]

When I coach endurance leaders, I ask, "What will get in the way of achieving our goals together?" It might be a very intense time at work, an extended holiday out of the country, or regular distractions such as frequent work travel. Then I ask, "How can we plan for those? What accommodations do we need to make to set coaching up for success? Will we need more time to achieve our outcome? Do we need an accountability plan to help you stay on track?"

Articulating these obstacles does two things. First, it helps endurance leaders be thoughtful and intentional about their goals and the realities that can get in their way. Second, it gives them ownership and agency over managing those obstacles when they occur, allowing for more success and limiting derailment.

Identify Obstacles

How can you identify these obstacles?

- *Be willing to revise your plans.* Recognize the interplay between your mission and the realities of your life and work. Kalisha's initial training plan had her working toward readiness for a promotion in two years. However, she hoped to expand her family in that period, which made her reconsider her timeline. She extended her timeline one extra year to accommodate.
- *Ask others.* Sometimes, the people around us can see the obstacles before us more clearly than we can. Not unlike uncovering blind spots, getting feedback from those who know you or have a different view of the organization can help you see the boulder around the corner.
- *Do your research.* Sometimes, obtaining statistical or historical data can inform your perspective and timeline. For example, Kalisha might ask her boss what the typical length of time someone in the company is in a vice president role before they are seen as promotion-eligible (and if it is different for women than men). That might help plan for disruptions.

You cannot prepare for every scenario, but when you build known or probable obstacles into the training plan, you are less likely to be thrown off by their emergence. You will be better equipped to stay anchored in your mission, remain true to your identity, and not lose momentum or get discouraged on your path to long-term success.

Coach's Questions ▬ ▬ ▬ ▬ ▬ ▬ ▬ ▬ ▬

- What obstacles do you anticipate as you implement your training plan over the next one to two years? If you don't know, how can you find out?

- Looking at your current obstacles, what changes do you need to make to achieve your long-term outcomes? How might your identity need to shift to help you work through those obstacles?

- How will you get support when those obstacles occur? In other words, what will buoy you through these disruptions so you can maintain your energy and motivation to get back in the race?

Training Plan

- You've already mapped out your leadership mission and set your training plan. Now, think about your life: work, family, health, community, and spiritual. In the table below, identify the obstacles that might affect your ability to meet those goals. Of course, five- and ten-year obstacles may be difficult to determine, but just thinking about these things can help you better prepare now.

- Plan strategies to help you overcome those obstacles. These might be behavioral strategies as well as emotional, physical, and social ones.

Goal	Obstacle(s)	Strategy
10+ years:		
5-10 years:		
2-5 years:		
6 months – 2 years:		
0-6 months:		

PART III

Excel In Execution

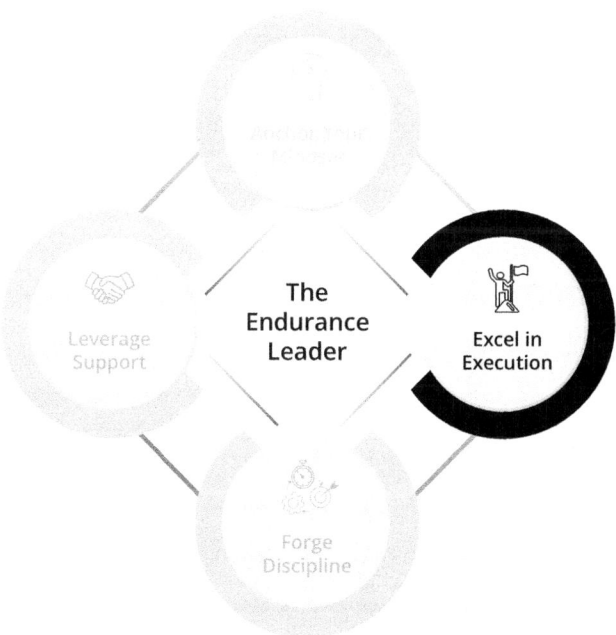

Chapter 6

Train Every Day

The only reason I'm able to do all the things I do
and to keep on top of a busy schedule
without getting too stressed is because I stay fit.

SIR RICHARD BRANSON

The Just Do It Mantra

When you hear "Just do it," you likely think of the fitness giant Nike. Nike incorporated this phrase into its brand strategy in 1987, and it still works today—you can probably picture the Nike swoosh now. Why does such a simple phrase have such intense meaning? Possibly because when a directive is prefaced with the word just, it seems like nothing should stop us. How could we *not* just do it? It springs us into action and compels us to move, do something, anything. And while that can be great (especially when that activity means buying more Nike products), it doesn't necessarily build endurance.

Endurance means repeating that just-do-it mantra every day—whether you feel like it or not. It is a spirit of commitment to something longer term, something nobler, than a momentary sentiment that compels the athlete/leader to invest in themselves, day after day—even when it is inconvenient. I'll share a few examples.

A Daily Commitment To Excellence

My friend Elisabetta (Betta) Villa is a world-class triathlete, dominating the sport with consistent top-three finishes in her age group at the Ironman World Championship over the past several years. She is also one of the fastest female marathoners in Italy, winning the 2020 Verdi Marathon—at age 48—with a time of 2:56:03 (two hours, fifty-six minutes, and three seconds). She is also the mother of two boys with active schedules and the founder of a nonprofit that teaches school-age children how to compete in triathlons.

For Betta, she could easily find an excuse not to train—her schedule is full even before she fits in her ten to fourteen hours per week of training. But for her, the training allows her to succeed in her other endeavors. And, as she says, training every day just feels good. This is a sentiment I often hear from endurance athletes, that training is akin to brushing their teeth—they can't get through the day without doing it. You may think this is an innate love of athletics, but this is an adopted mindset.

Betta will tell you she was not athletic when she was younger and only discovered running and endurance sports in adulthood. She was not born with a disposition any different from yours and mine—instead, she developed a discipline around exercise. It takes a lot of ruthless prioritization, scheduling, and effort, but she makes it happen. She remains committed to continuing to pursue her sport by training every day.

Murphy is an endurance leader who excels in execution through a daily commitment to training. Murphy has experienced enormous success, landing his first executive position in his mid-twenties and now, in his thirties, acting as the CEO of a successful company.

Murphy talks about the importance of investing in his physical, spiritual and mental health to the success of his business. In fact, the busier he is, the more important these personal investments become. Murphy wakes before his young family and takes time for physical activity, prayer/ meditation, and goal reflection. This consistency gives him the clarity and grounding he needs to deliver in a big job every day. Like Betta, Murphy is committed to training every day.

Clarifying Priorities

You might be wondering, "But how do I find the time? I'm so busy." You're not alone; many people have difficulty figuring out how to prioritize commitment to their leadership development and personal and professional goals. Work can become all-demanding if we let it. But allow me to offer a reframe: who has an abundance or a paucity of time? We all have the same time. Leaders who train every day prioritize their leadership growth and make the time to focus on it.

The term ruthless prioritization gained popularity from Sheryl Sandberg, former COO of Meta (formerly Facebook). While she was talking about idea generation, the use of the term has expanded to refer to time management. By creating a laser-like focus on what is essential to achieving our mission-driven identity and longer-term goals, you will get clear on what needs to be done every day to get there—and what doesn't.

A quote from longtime leadership expert Stephen Covey is, "The key is not to prioritize what is on your schedule, but to schedule your priorities."[29] In other words, by taking charge of our time, we can set up the space to execute what we know is critical to our long-term leadership success.

Ways to ruthlessly prioritize include the following:

- *Start by doing only what only you can do.* For example, who can build your leadership strength and longevity besides you? No one. Who can run that daily 8 a.m. meeting that prevents you from getting time to focus on your leadership growth? Likely any number of people. So, empower others to do the things that are on your plate that you don't have to do (like run a daily meeting) to make time for the things you must do to achieve your goals.

- *Maintain strict boundaries.* Every time you say yes to something, determine what you will say no to. Without doing so, you are engaging in magical thinking, assuming your plate will get bigger if you put more stuff on it. If you try that the next time you have a plate of food, you will quickly see how poorly that thinking plays out. Adding more activities does not make you more productive, effective, engaged, or happier. When at least part of your focus involves what is most important to you, you will be more motivated to continue the long and exciting road ahead of you as a leader.

The Importance Of Tiny Gains

Endurance leaders find ways to deliver against their leadership goals every day. It doesn't mean they take massive strides daily; it is quite the opposite. It's the small efforts that matter. What if you could get even 1 percent closer to your ultimate mission without much work? It really can be that easy. It's a matter of perspective—and commitment.

We introduced the concept of Minimum Viable Effort (MVE) previously. BJ Fogg describes the importance of small steps critical to MVE and meaningful change: "Make it tiny. To create a new habit, you must first simplify the behavior. Make it tiny, even ridiculous. A good tiny behavior is easy to do—and fast."[30]

This may be a foreign concept for most of us when our organizations talk about BHAGs (Big, Hairy, Audacious Goals) or quantum-level changes deemed critical for winning in the marketplace. For Betta and Murphy, the changes to their daily training regimen are likely small and consistent and, over time, result in significant gains in their performance, whether in a triathlon or a boardroom.

A fitting example of MVE is the learn-to-run program called From Couch to 5K, developed in the 1990s by a British runner trying to get his mom to start running.[31] It begins with an assumption that the participant is doing zero running. It starts with short run-walk intervals a few days per week and gradually builds to a 5km distance race at the end of the sixth week. The program has been so successful it is now recommended by Britain's National Health Service.[32] (For Fogg, this is probably still too much effort—he might suggest that on Day 1, you transition from sitting on the couch to standing up, and that's all.)

MVE And Daily Training

Let's combine MVE and the notion of training every day using MVE. Let's say you are a leader trying to become more influential in meetings. How can you train every day to get better at that, particularly if you aren't in a meeting every single day? Perhaps it requires a reframe.

Rather than restricting the place to train to only meetings, let's look at other places where you could practice being more influential every day. What is the behavioral change you could make in daily interactions that would enhance your influence? Perhaps it starts with offering one well-placed question in at least one interpersonal interaction every day. That might strengthen your influence by 1 percent or more. Once you've mastered that, perhaps you move on to the subsequent 1 percent gain, such as seeking out someone else's point of view. Again, the small steps are what make the difference.

Training to be an endurance leader isn't the equivalent of sprinting down the street every few days. It's the dedicated, consistent commitment to put effort into your daily training plan. It may not be noteworthy, but it can bring considerable returns to your long-term success.

Coach's Questions ▰ ▰ ▰ ▰ ▰ ▰ ▰ ▰ ▰

- What are some MVEs you could implement for your most important goals? Where could you make a 1 percent investment in getting better every day?

- What gets in the way of your daily training? Is there a way to delegate more, set firmer boundaries, or increase some other personal discipline that would give you even a brief amount of time to focus on your leadership goals?

- How can you practice your leadership goals every day? If the goal you're working on doesn't have an environment for practice that is available daily, how can you modify your goal (a 1 percent shift) to create a space where you could practice? Remember, endurance athletes train every day; even if they must modify their plan, they find a way to do something that gets them closer to their goal.

Training Plan

- Expanding your chart from Chapter 5, add in a 1 percent improvement goal. Add as much specificity as possible to make it more meaningful and likely. Consider:

  - What does 1 percent better look like?

  - Where/how will you focus on that improvement (what environment or situation, who is present)?

  - What will others observe?

  - Who will give you feedback to help you improve?

  - How will you ensure you get a chance to practice every day?

Goal	Strategy	What Does 1% Better Look Like?
10+ years:		
5-10 years:		
2-5 years:		
6 months – 2 years:		
0-6 months:		

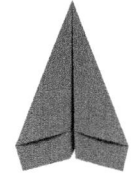

Chapter 7

Use The Action-Reflection Cycle

We do not learn from experience;
we learn from reflecting on experience.
John Dewey

The Power Of A Pause

I have a remarkable client, David Lee Windecher. David, a criminal defense lawyer, started a nonprofit focused on working with law enforcement and the criminal justice system to eliminate recidivism. David's history growing up in deep poverty and subsequent experiences being incarcerated multiple times left him distrustful of many people, particularly law enforcement and the criminal justice system. This posed a challenge for him since these are the people with whom he interacts every day.

To make the nonprofit successful, he must appeal to these very groups and be seen as a trusted partner. When David and I began coaching work together, he told me he often felt triggered by interactions he would have with police officers, lawyers, and judges. In those moments, he would frequently react caustically or cynically, undermining his efforts to work successfully with these groups.

I suggested David reflect on his feelings and reactions after such moments. I asked him to write down what happened, what emotions were stirred, and where they came from. I also encouraged him to take one breath before reacting in these triggering situations to give himself a moment to think before responding. When we next met, David started our session by exclaiming, "The stuff you're teaching me is starting to pan out!" He told me that he was getting triggered the day before as he was defending someone in court. His responses (actions) were making things worse.

Suddenly, David stopped and counted to four in his head (reflection). This gave him enough time to identify his feelings, recognize they were about his past and not relevant to the case, and refocus his attention on the facts of the case. Those few seconds helped him deliver an excellent result for his client. Over the next several months, David strengthened his four-second strategy, resulting in fewer emotional reactions and more significant influence and impact in crucial work and personal situations. Reflection worked.

Pairing Action With Reflection

The importance of reflecting on action is longstanding. It is embedded in the teachings of the thirteenth-century poet Rumi and traverses the work of psychology greats John Dewey, Jean Piaget, Kurt Lewin, and David Kolb, to name just a few. A few of the most cited models are the Gibbs Reflective Cycle (see Figure 10) and Driscoll's 1994 model "What? So What? Now What?" (based on Terry Borton's original questions in 1970).[33]

Figure 10. Gibbs Reflective Cycle

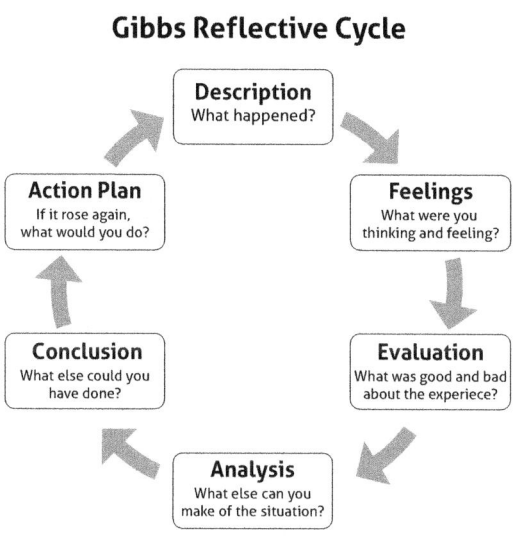

Slowing down thinking can be difficult, as time and work demands can pull you toward reactive decisions, particularly ones that might seem familiar and easy. But as we can see from endurance athletes and leaders, engaging in reflective cycles is critical to helping us stay on track toward our powerful goals.

As a coach, asking busy leaders to reflect at the end of the day or week on some action we've targeted will inevitably lead to few meaningful results. Too many things happen between the activity and the reflection, and the leader can't remember it accurately, or it seems like old news. Instead, getting leaders to reflect immediately after an action or activity—or, better yet, during the action—results in much greater integrity in the reflection process. So, in this model, I deem it an action-reflection process rather than just a reflection process.

Why do these processes work? Because the action-reflection process allows us to move from reaction to analysis, helping us to make better decisions. In Daniel Kahneman's book *Thinking, Fast and Slow*,[34] he differentiates between System I and System II thinking. System I is instinctive, often unconscious, and emotional. This is the default mechanism we use when we are triggered (as David was) or when we don't want to be challenged to think in more complex ways. System II thinking is slower, more deliberate, and more logical. Reflection allows us time to slow down our thinking, moving from System I to System II.

Action-Reflection And Performance

Reflection in sports is not a nice thing to have, but it is a must. At the 2020 Tokyo Olympics, British synchronized divers Tom Daley and Matty Lee won the gold medal with a spectacular dive. If you watch a video of that dive, you will see how perfectly timed they had to be to get it exactly right.[35] That type of precision can only occur through consistent cycles of action followed by immediate reflection, several times an hour during practice.

Reflection need not take a long time—it may only be a moment when you are as skilled as these athletes—but it is necessary to fine-tune the approach. They couldn't wait until the end of the day or week to have that reflection. Can you imagine what would be at risk if these athletes did not take time to reflect on their actions?

In Faull and Cropley's 2009 article on reflective practices, they found that "…reflective practice can be used to holistically aid athletic performance. Evidence was found for an increase in self-awareness and evaluative skills and supports the notion that reflective practice should be considered as a component for athlete development."[36] In other words, athletes improve their performance when utilizing the action-reflection cycle. Betta Villa talks about the importance of reflection: "I write in my diary every day. I write down my training sessions and my feelings about my training sessions. It keeps me focused on what I'm doing and what I need to do."[37]

To remain focused on the goals in front of them, athletes must make time to think about their performance and process their feelings about it. Not every training session goes well, while some are spectacular. They know that if they ride the highs and lows of a single moment, they can potentially develop unrealistic expectations or put themselves into a doom spiral. By properly processing thoughts and emotions, athletes move into an analytic space that allows more objectivity and the ability to plan for future performance.

You may be thinking, "OK, but these are professionals. Their job is to perform at these levels and make time for reflection. But I don't have that kind of time." I would argue that if you want to become an endurance leader, your job also requires this kind of dedication. Those athletes do not have more time, but what they have in spades is a deep and abiding commitment to their success.

Research shows that reflection may be a distinguishing characteristic of long-term leadership success. Lanaj (2019) found that when leaders engaged in daily self-reflection, they experienced less depletion and heightened work engagement.[38] Citrin et al. published an article on long-serving CEOs in *Harvard Business Review*. They found, "Actively developing the ability to step back, reflect, and recalibrate in view of early experiences expands a CEO's tool kit, improves pattern recognition, and increases speed to action."[39]

The evidence is clear: Reflective practices help high performers achieve more remarkable performances. As an aspiring endurance leader, you will benefit from reflective practices that help you remain aligned with your goals. Luckily, your reflection time may not need to be as immediate as an Olympic diver between dives. But it can also easily fall by the wayside if you don't create discipline around it.

Build Reflection Into Existing Strategies

One of the easiest and most effective ways to engage in the action-reflection cycle is to build it into your existing practices:

- *Meditation.* Meditation (spiritual or not) has myriad positive effects on humans. In endurance athletes, it reduces stress, builds confidence, enhances self-esteem, improves focus, creates energy, and builds endurance.[40] For many people, meditation is a routine that helps them build focus and clarity in their day. If this is a practice you already utilize, it might be a perfect place to engage in some action-reflection work. Take 10–20 percent of your meditation time to think about your endurance leader goals, what has gone well, and where you might want to focus your efforts to become even more effective. Deep breathing and focusing on growth, rather than errors, will encourage positive experiences of the practice and enhance self-esteem and self-efficacy.

- *Exercise.* The evidence regarding the mental and physical benefits of regular exercise is incontrovertible. If you are an exerciser, depending on your activity of choice, exercise time can provide the perfect opportunity to reflect on your leadership goals. The next time you are about to head out the door for a bike ride or walk, perhaps ditch the earbuds (at least for a few minutes) and spend at least a few minutes thinking about your goals. Set a timer on your watch or phone to start and stop to give yourself time to focus on other things or nothing at all, which is also a vital workout priority.

- *Journaling.* Journaling has emerged as an integral part of many people's lives, including top executives: writing down thoughts helps them create clarity, process feelings, challenge their thinking, and move through the action-reflection cycle more quickly. Writing things down also helps people get things done. From beautiful paper journals to journaling apps to phone talk-to-text, getting your thoughts down has never been easier or more convenient.

- *Contemporaneous reflection.* As we saw in David's example, there are often opportunities to reflect throughout our workday. Sometimes, immediately activating the action-reflection cycle is prudent and necessary to keep us from doing something we might regret later. But those moments aside, there are likely other opportunities throughout the day when you might walk away from an interaction and think,

"Hm, I probably could have done better there." By stopping and sitting with that thought, giving yourself three to five minutes to work through the action-reflection process, you might turn a quick observation into a growth opportunity (and you can write it down in your brand-new journal).

- *Apps, apps, apps.* There are myriad apps ready and waiting to help you with your reflection processes: meditation, journaling, and focus apps. No matter what you want to accomplish, you can make it happen—for less than a fancy cup of coffee.
- *Support from others.* Other people can be an excellent medium for reflection. Whether you are part of a leadership development initiative, have supportive peers, or use a coach, engaging others in discussions about your development is a natural way to reflect.

Coach's Questions ━ ━ ━ ━ ━ ━ ━ ━ ━

- How can the action-reflection cycle help you stay aligned with your goals?

- What strategies can you employ to make the action-reflection cycle a natural part of your leadership activity?

- For some people, the process can lead to self-criticism and negative evaluation of progress. What can you do to keep the process positive and self-affirming?

- What will you lose without a regular process of action and reflection?

Training Plan

- Review some action-reflection suggestions above and pick one that works for you. Print it out and stick it somewhere where you can see it easily and regularly.

- Build a realistic strategy and cadence for your action-reflection process. Will you journal at the end of each day? Will you reflect in the morning during your meditation time? Find the lowest friction process you can and do it.

- Take small steps to build the process into your daily routine. How much time is reasonable to spend on these activities? (Remember the 1 percent better rule from James Clear.)

Chapter 8

Run The Mile You're In

Whatever the present moment contains,
accept it as if you had chosen it.
Always work with it, not against it.

ECKHART TOLLE

A Needed Reframe

Some time ago, I completed a half-Ironman race. I had been training for six months and was optimistic about my performance, hoping to beat my personal record (PR) for that distance. While I'd prepared smartly (in my mid-50s at that time, remaining injury-free was more critical than my race time), I'd had some tightness in my right hamstring and had been trying to be very careful not to overuse it in the final weeks leading up to the race.

In triathlon, the order of events is swim, bike, and run. I had a good swim and an excellent bike portion of the race, so I felt good as I transitioned to my 13.1-mile run. I started with a strong run pace, but in mile two, I suddenly felt my right quadricep muscle cramp. It wasn't terrible, but I knew I needed to slow down and give it a minute to work itself out.

So, I stopped running momentarily and attempted to stretch the quadricep. It was the wrong thing to do. My opposing muscle—that pesky hamstring I'd been trying to protect—wrenched into a horrible seizure. If I moved that leg in any direction, it would make it worse. As I spent several minutes waiting and lightly stretching, I could feel the clock ticking and my goal of a PR slipping away.

I realized I needed to reframe my approach quickly; my PR goal now seemed impossible and pursuing it would only put me at risk of further injury. Despite all that was happening with me and around me, I stopped and thought, "What am I out here for?" I reminded myself that my goal was to do my best and foster my pursuit of health and longevity; I wasn't out here to win anything.

So, I changed my goal from pursuing a PR to finishing the race as best I could. I started walking slowly at first. People were passing me all over the place, and for a few minutes, I felt a twinge of self-pity for having to switch to walking. But as I passed through throngs of cheering spectators, I thought, "This is fun—I usually don't get to appreciate all this support and celebration." A few moments later, the first female finisher crossed the finish line. People were going wild, and I could cheer and whoop for her in a way I wouldn't have had I been running, as I would have been too focused on my performance to pay attention to her.

Getting out of my head for a few minutes helped buoy my spirits and fuel my newly reframed approach to the race. I decided to try a slow jog for about 100 meters. When I could do that without the leg seizing up, I aimed for the three-mile sign, which was not too far ahead of me. I got there and still felt OK. I decided to try to speed up, ever so slightly, to the next water stop (around mile four). Still OK. I continued to set goals for the space between the water stops (at approximately every mile).

My goals were less about increasing my pace and more about keeping good form—proper heel strike, forward lean, weight distribution, and breathing. When I crossed the finish line, I discovered—much to my surprise—that I had beaten my personal record by three minutes! My change of focus from running the fastest race I could to running the mile I was in helped me run fast enough to achieve my goal (albeit unwittingly).

While setting small goals during a race is not unusual for me (nor for many endurance athletes), reframing a goal under adversity is different. It requires the athlete to get outside of their situation and engage in what is known as metacognition (thinking about thinking) while under duress. By taking a moment to evaluate what thoughts and feelings are controlling them, the athlete can wrest control of their mental game. They can then choose to think more positively, change their game plan, and keep their negative thoughts under control.

Reframing Is A Discipline

What allows people to endure? Is it that they are better programmed in their brain and emotional regulatory (limbic) system? Not likely; endurance athletes and endurance leaders are not superhuman. They are not born with higher systems of pain tolerance than other people. Instead, they have learned mental strategies to help them shift from feeling sorry for themselves or discouraged during difficult situations to an attitude of, "What can I do to improve my situation and get closer to my goal?"

Rutledge et al.'s study of subjective well-being (2014) found that mood, outlook, and stress levels are related to expectations and current reality.[41] To paraphrase their conclusion, our brains react to reality positively or negatively depending on our expectations.

Endurance leaders and athletes excel at recognizing that momentary happiness or unhappiness is a temporal state. They acknowledge those feelings but put them into the context of the broader realities of long-term goals. They focus on what they can control right now, a strategy that builds optimism and energy because it fosters a sense of agency and self-control. This takes discipline, but it is achievable with proper focus and commitment.

Longtime mountain bike champion Rebecca Rusch describes the phenomenon: "Whenever I get down and catch myself with negative thoughts, I pretend I'm saying those things aloud to another person. I ask myself, "Would you ever say, 'Well, it looks like you're really blowing up; your day is over,' to a training partner who is struggling? Of course not! You'd tell him, 'Keep pushing and just make it through the next five minutes.' Or maybe you'd say, 'Eat, drink, and hang in there until the next aid station.'

Going through this exercise helps me replace negative thoughts with positive ones. I guess what I'm saying is that you've got to be kind to yourself. If you are kind to yourself, most of the time, you'll get through the dark spot in a better mood and without wasting precious energy ruminating."[42]

In the first months of 2022, as the world struggled through a global health pandemic, Weaving Influence CEO Becky Robinson wrote a *SmartBrief* article titled: "A Crisis Is Not a Marathon—But It Is a Call for Endurance." She applied the principle of running the mile you're in to leadership, saying, "As a leader facing multiple business challenges, I am paralyzed when I worry too much about next quarter. Long-term planning is critical, but I'll find the strength to endure if I show up for what's needed in this moment."[43]

Talking with Murphy (whom you met earlier), he shared a similar philosophy when faced with a major crisis in his company: "A few years ago, our business was severely disrupted by hurricanes. It was easy to get discouraged. But instead, we stepped away from 'woe is me' and stepped into the messiness, focusing on doing the next best thing. Rather than getting swept up in the fears of the long term, we got up and got after the daily focus. *Calm is contagious.*"[44] (What a great phrase.) As Murphy eloquently said, the only way to create calm in a crisis is to ensure that your mental energy stays focused and directed.

Escaping Survival Mode

Uncertainty seems to be on the minds of every leader these days. Business leaders constantly adjust to new business realities despite uncertainties and volatility, such as global geopolitical issues, changing market forces, rapidly evolving technologies like artificial intelligence (AI), and climate change. When things are uncertain, it can be easy to hunker down and stick with what we know, taking a wait-and-see approach before moving in any direction. But there are two challenges with that mindset:

- *It keeps us stuck.* When we stick only to what we know, we narrow our thinking and overlook alternative or unfamiliar ways of approaching a situation that could help us reach the next decision point. We become passive, waiting to be convinced that a solution will move us forward, rather than being active experimenters ready to fail fast and learn from our mistakes. This can be likened to Carol Dweck's fixed (versus growth) mindset.[45]

- *It activates preservationist systems in the body.* Our fight-or-flight mechanism is so biologically ordered that it is immediate and unconscious; our limbic system decides that there is a threat, and we automatically respond accordingly. However, the thinking that activates our limbic system may be more programmable. If we expect environmental threats, we are more likely to pay attention to them than any positive or less threatening information that might be available. In other words, we see the world through smog-colored glasses rather than rose-colored ones.

  For example, let's assume your company has a hiring and promotion freeze due to current market uncertainty. You might say, "Well, I have no hope of getting promoted for the next year," so you may hunker down with your day-to-day responsibilities and hope the hiring freeze will end soon. (As an analogy, imagine running a race in a downpour and focusing only on the relentless rain, hoping it will stop.) Or perhaps you start looking for a job elsewhere (which might mean quitting the race altogether in our race metaphor).

In either condition, you may become discouraged about your organization and look for evidence that they are not loyal to their employees or that the culture is not great. These ways of thinking may protect you from investing in the company as a survival technique. Still, they do nothing to ensure you continue growing your skills or pushing yourself up in visibility, creativity, and leadership.

Learning To Run The Mile You're In

To help you move from survival mode to running the mile you're in, here are a few steps:

- *Directly challenge your thinking.* Like Rebecca Rusch, sometimes it can be helpful to make your inside-your-head voice alive on the outside. If you engage in negative self-talk, ask yourself, "Would I ever talk to a colleague or friend this way?" Saying these things out loud or writing them down can help us identify their ridiculousness. Challenge yourself to talk to yourself like a friend would, "Can you stick with it just another few minutes/hours/weeks? I bet you can. You are so strong." This kind of mental reframe can be critical when you find yourself starting to get sucked into the black hole of negativity and self-preservation.

- *Focus on what you can control.* Part of what makes long, protracted periods of uncertainty so painful is the feeling that we do not have control. What becomes our focus is getting to the end of that lack of certainty. (Picture yourself in the backseat of life's longest car ride, saying, "Are we there yet?") If we can instead turn our attention to what we have control over, we activate our sense of agency—the ability to be self-directed and intrinsically motivated.[46] Applying this to the promotion issue above, you might focus on minor changes in your leadership approach, such as becoming a better coach to your team members or investing more in your peer network. In this way, you are not waiting for external motivators to drive you forward but rather remaining present in the moment and what good you can do now.

- *Make learning the goal, not winning.* Remember James Clear's advice on setting goals? Start with identity, and let the behaviors follow. When we place goals before identity, we quickly create a win-lose dynamic for ourselves. During times of uncertainty, we can get discouraged when it is less clear where we are on that path and worry our identity is at risk. Instead, if we focus on using our sense of agency, we can engage in self-directed and intentional learning and reduce the unhelpful noise of evaluating our performance. As learners, we can turn the uncertainty into questions like, "How does this situation challenge me to think/act differently?" or "How can I be the best leader possible given current conditions?"

- *Leverage intermittent rewards.* Part of the "Are we there yet?" agony is due to feeling like our ultimate reward, the finish line, is not in sight. Keeping our energy and motivation up can be difficult when circumstances are adverse or uncertainty is high. Setting mini-goals with micro-rewards for success helps us focus on progress, pulling us away from survival mode and back into a mindset where we can thrive. So, if your mini-goal is to be more coach-like with your team, perhaps you set a reward for yourself by surveying team members to learn how your coach-like behaviors have helped them. Or maybe you reward yourself for building your peer network by having an enjoyable dinner with some of your new colleagues. It might not lead to a promotion—yet—but it might help you feel good about your path to getting there.

Coach's Questions ▬ ▬ ▬ ▬ ▬ ▬ ▬ ▬ ▬

- What uncertainties make it difficult to keep your energy and focus right now?

- What parts of this can/do you control?

- What steps can you take to focus on the elements you can control (run the mile you are in)?

- What rewards will help you keep up your energy, motivation, and agency-focused learning?

Training Plan

- Imagine yourself in a running race with the fulfillment of your ultimate mission as the finish line. Where are you in the race? Are you at the starting line? Picture yourself on the journey. What tools/resources do you have with you?

- Imagine you are now experiencing some obstacles on your route. Perhaps it is uncertainty (unsure where the road leads) or adversity (the weather has turned foul). What can you tell yourself/do right now to keep your feet moving one in front of the other?

- Reframe negative self-talk to positive, agency-focused thoughts to keep you centered on what you can control. What do you want to learn from this moment?

- Set small rewards to keep you focused on achieving mini-goals along your journey.

Chapter 9

Learn Pacing

If you're always racing to the next moment,
what's happening in this moment?
UNKNOWN

The Futility Of The Constant Sprint

I had a client, Nora, during a time when a global health crisis was impacting many businesses. Nora spent much of her workdays putting out fires, fielding crisis video meetings from company executives and clients, and managing constant changes to business priorities. She was not getting the time she needed with her direct reports to create the right operational tempo, reprioritize work demands, and engage in the creative processes necessary to propel the business forward.

Nora spent the first few months of this crisis trying to sprint through it, leaving her frazzled and exhausted. She was trying to do it all herself, sleeping too little and worrying too much. Nora and many others learned from this experience that there is no way to sprint through complex challenges and protracted uncertainty. It is unsustainable and will not lead us where we want to be—because no one knows precisely where and when the end will be.

To perform at our best and get great results over the long haul, we need to learn a little about the endurance athlete's concept of *pacing*.

Marathon runners know that if they let the speed of other runners affect them, they can start a race too fast, burn up their energy stores too quickly, and find themselves flagging by the race's end. They must manage their pace to execute their plan for a strong race.

Similarly, leaders like Nora can feel pressured by business imperatives, peer comparison, and a sense of urgency to keep a sprint pace for an indeterminate amount of time. The result can be burnout, health issues, and inferior performance. To overcome this, leaders must have a plan for how they and their teams can recover from sprint moments to keep their energy from getting wholly sapped. It doesn't mean leaders and teams won't ever need to sprint, but it's about managing that effort that is key for long-term success.

Pacing And Performance

Skorski and Abbiss define the endurance athlete concept of pacing as "The regulation of speed, power or energy expenditure throughout an exercise task," which is "extremely important in the optimization of performance."[47] By varying speed and intensity throughout an effort, athletes conserve their energy to be available when needed. A fantastic example of this is watching Katie Ledecky during her world-record performance in the 800-meter freestyle swim at the 2016 Olympics.[48] A key to her success was her controlled use of power and pacing, which she adjusted throughout the race by varying her kick. As the finish line drew closer, Katie transformed a steady, easy-looking kick into a powerful, controlled one. As a result, she broke a world record and dusted her nearest competitor by eleven seconds (an eternity in the swimming world).

If you have ever run a race of any distance, you know what happens when you ignore the principles of pacing. If you start too fast and try to sprint the entire effort, you experience either physiological or mental fatigue or both. As an endurance athlete, I have often practiced pacing regularly in the weeks leading up to a running event. Yet, on race day, nerves and excitement sometimes get the best of me, and I start the race too fast. Inevitably, my pacing falters, and I pay the price in a disappointing finish time or, worse, injury.

When companies and leaders do not pace themselves during times of crisis, they can find themselves limping to the financial and competitive finish line. During that same global health crisis, David Solomon, the CEO of Goldman Sachs, famously said in February 2021 that remote work is "not a new normal … it's an aberration that we're going to correct as soon as possible."[49]

The problem was that the health crisis lasted longer than anticipated, and people had adjusted to remote work by then. Goldman's forced return-to-work policies resulted in large-scale defections when the job market improved several months later. Goldman attempted to sprint their way to a finish line that moved further out during the race, resulting in an unsustainable pace.

By contrast, DoorDash's CEO Tony Xu committed to providing financial assistance to health-related quarantined drivers, converting to a zero-contact delivery method, and adding 100,000 independent restaurant partners to their DashPass platform.[50] By adopting a marathon mentality, Xu created a manageable pace for his team, putting long-term goals (e.g., market capture) ahead of short-term wins and allowing him to build the tempo for success over time. The result? Massive revenue growth over the next several years[51] and solid growth potential.

Pacing And The Endurance Leader

A notable example of pacing is from Ellen, a third-generation CEO of a small family-owned manufacturing company. A fire occurred in one of Ellen's three production facilities some years ago. She and her team had to quickly double production in two other plants to make up for the losses, moving the plants to twenty-four-hour operations. The teams in those facilities had to work more hours for several weeks until the fire damage was repaired.

During this time, Ellen promised her team that when the crisis was over, she would provide employees an additional half day off for each pay period they worked during the crisis period. However, she also made a caveat: the time had to be used within the next six months. The goal was to reward their efforts and give them time to breathe and recover from putting in so much additional hard work and sacrifice. It wasn't just an extra holiday but an effort to move from a sprint mentality back to a manageable pace. She recognized that everyone would perform better in the long term if they spent some time working not quite as hard for a few subsequent weeks.

Ellen, too, needed to manage her leadership pace during this time. The company and the facilities are not just a business for Ellen; the buildings are a part of her family's history, and the people in the company are her extended family. She worked countless hours, showing up day and night to offer a hand and encourage her staff. However, she realized that if she did not pace herself, she would be at risk of burning herself out, and she would inadvertently encourage her staff to overdo it by modeling a sprint mentality.

Admittedly, she did not give herself the same time off benefit but took an extended holiday once the damaged facility was back in operation. What were the benefits of this approach? Ellen's business sustained little financial loss during the plant repair, and because the repair allowed for some opportunities to upgrade equipment, the plant increased efficiency, improving earnings substantially over the following three quarters. While the cost of additional time off for employees was high, the company had *fewer* absences than average during the operational downtime, which boosted productivity. Moreover, she had little turnover, and the annual culture survey reflected high marks; people felt and saw Ellen's loyalty to them and commitment to getting to a successful solution fast.

By varying from sprint effort (intense hours during the facility repair) to easy effort (holidays and days off), Ellen was betting that her team would be more successful throughout the year, even with the fire. She was right, as the survey scores and increased earnings showed.

Learning To Pace

You may benefit from learning how to pace to meet your endurance leader challenges effectively. Consider these strategies:

- *Build your base.* Many endurance athletes spend most of their training time at a level of effort that is challenging but sustainable, a concept known as building your base.[52] Try these strategies to ensure you have a robust base:
  - *Find a sustainable pace and effort level.* Create a cadence for work and nonwork activities that does not exhaust you (or your team). Plan out rest and recovery periods and convey those to people who can help you stay accountable. As you ruthlessly prioritize, ensure that your pacing strategy is considered in those priorities. Jimmy and his team put together a strategic plan for building the hospital that was aggressive but realistic. They regularly calibrated against their goals to determine if they were on pace. They planned for lull periods and planned vacations and teambuilding activities for those times to keep people grounded and refreshed.
  - *Stay consistent and hold your ground.* Plan goals and stick to them, building in time for unanticipated demands. Give yourself the freedom and flexibility to say no or not now to maintain focus and a manageable but challenging pace. During the hospital project, there were constant disruptions to the construction

schedule; Jimmy had to know when to shift timelines, push back, and challenge the builders to stay on schedule.

- *Find ways to take breaks and recharge.* Build and keep your energy high through adequate sleep, self-care, support, and reflection time. Remember, human resilience is critical to long-term leadership and business success.[53] Jimmy continued his ultramarathon training during the project. His view was, "The times when I can least afford to train are when I need most to train." It is a critical element of his self-care and helps him focus and manage stress.

- *Pick up the pace when needed.* No matter how much planning and anticipating you do, the unpredictable will happen. You need to have some fuel left in the tank to perform well when it does. It is the work equivalent of the surprise big hill at mile eighteen of a 26.2-mile marathon. If you have been working too hard for the first seventeen miles, you will not have what it takes to pick up your pace and get over the hill effectively. Strategies to develop a differentiated yet sustainable pace include the following:

  - *When more work effort is necessary, be explicit about its intensity and duration.* When you are charged with changing focus to solve an immediate business demand, clarify how much time, energy, and effort you and your team can devote to such an effort. Create boundaries around your time and manage others' expectations so that you all have a demarcated finish line. This makes these intense efforts psychologically manageable.

  - *Create cycles of extra effort to build strength and mental agility.* Many endurance coaches preach against training in what is called the grey zone, in other words, exercising at an intensity that is moderately difficult but does not allow the athlete to adjust to a harder effort easily.[54] Instead of training in the grey zone, they recommend the athlete intentionally hold her effort back, then pick up the pace when a more strenuous effort is needed. As a result, the athlete learns to sustain harder work at higher levels of effort over time. As Jimmy did with the hospital project, extra effort for you might mean taking full advantage of a business or market slowdown to give yourself and your team members more time to spend in teambuilding, learning, and development or using well-deserved time off. This will help you gain strength and make you more resilient and productive when the business calls for a ramp-up. This can also inoculate you against getting sucked into what researcher and professor Brené Brown calls "exhaustion as status symbol."[55]

- *Recommit to discipline—often.* The desire to act quickly to get things done is much like that starting line at the marathon, where many people start too fast. Remind yourself that short-term firefighting approaches may help you win the day, but they aren't going to sustain your leadership for the long term.
- *Face it: we are not great sprinters.* The world's fastest sprinters spend a relatively small percentage of their training time sprinting. Yet many of us may believe that our companies need us to sprint 24/7. To help us maintain a realistic viewpoint, we must remember that the long view is the one that ultimately wins the endurance race. Many organizations now recognize that long-term performance has a significantly higher value for shareholders and employees than a short-term focus.[56] To keep the proper perspective:
    - *Remember that we can – and should – sprint from time to time, and then STOP sprinting.* Sprint when you must, but before you do so, plan to find your way back to a more manageable pace that allows for recovery and rebuilding strength.
    - *Regularly assess yourself and your team.* The costs of continuous sprinting can be devastating for an athlete, resulting in overtraining and injury. Yet we may try to convince ourselves we can keep up an untenable pace without adverse effects. The reality is that we

are every bit as susceptible to injury as the athlete. In the case of work, continuous sprinting can lead to burnout, lack of clarity and direction, poor decision-making, and suboptimal outcomes. Ask yourself and your team regularly, "What problem are we solving?" "Why are we doing this?" and "Is this a sustainable pace?" Consult with your team, boss, and family to check your assumptions so you do not overtrain and risk business or personal health.

There is no such thing as perfect regarding your ideal pace, but there is such a thing as better. Aim for that. I predict that doing so will make you faster, fitter, and more excited about the work in front of you.

Coach's Questions

- How much of your time, inside and out of work, feels like a sprint?

- What risks exist if you continue to sprint at your current intensity/ duration (e.g., poor health, lack of sleep, burnout, anxiety)?

- What rewards do you get (overtly or unconsciously) from sprinting? For example, "The company rewards my efforts to produce more with less," or "It's important to me to feel like the pacesetter for the team."

- How can you manage risks and rewards effectively to build a sustainable pace that ensures you stay true to your long-term goals? What do you need to say no to or yes to?

Training Plan

- Evaluate how much time you spend in sprint mode versus running at a manageable pace: Review your calendar for the last two weeks and assign each activity either an S for sprint or M for manageable. If the ratio feels lopsided (more than 20 percent of your activities are an S), plan how you can and will adjust.

- Identify the resources and strategies that will help you spend more time at a manageable pace. One strategy might be to do a better job of delegating daily tasks to team members. Another is to find someone to hold you accountable for downtime on your calendar for strategy work and thinking time. Another is to outsource tasks at home like housecleaning or grocery shopping.

- Reevaluate your pacing regularly. Check in with your team, colleagues, boss, friends, or family to determine if you are modeling at the right pace. Also, calibrate against your long-term leadership goals. Are you progressing toward them, or are you sidelined due to overuse from too many sprints?

Chapter 10

Recover

━━ ━━ ━━ ━━ ━━ ━━

Take care of your body. It's the only place you have to live.
Jim Rohn

The "Iron Cowboy"

In the triathlon world, there exists a man of legend, James Lawrence, aka "Iron Cowboy." Lawrence became famous for doing something understood to be impossible: in 2015, at age forty, he completed fifty Ironman-distance triathlons in fifty states in fifty days. For those of you playing along at home, that's 120 miles of swimming, 5,600 miles of biking, and 1,310 miles of running! Unbelievable, right? It's not as impressive as his feat of *doubling* that distance in 2021, with 100 Ironman-distance homemade races in 100 days. His resilience and ability to perform under these circumstances have inspired thousands. And he claimed to do all of it to support worthy causes.[57]

These feats were possible for Lawrence due to the intense recovery that followed each day's achievement: two hours in a hyperbaric oxygen chamber every night, compression boots, red-light therapy, and scores of massages. In addition, he used controversial vitamin-intensive IVs, which are banned in formal racing events under anti-doping regulations.

Lawrence attests that, while he broke through unimaginable pain levels and pushed the limits of his endurance ability, he also endured significant injury. As soon as the event was over, he announced his retirement from the sport of triathlon. In an interview, he said, "It was a challenge that lasted a quarter of a year, and I think I was almost in a crisis state. Your mind is so powerful that it puts you in a state of [survival]. It tries to protect you from what's been happening. Then, when you finish, you start to feel all those things that your mind's been sheltering from you."[58]

Iron Cowboy's feats of human perseverance were newsworthy but unsustainable for most. He had access to resources that the everyday athlete doesn't have. While he took little rest during these event periods, it led to an extreme outcome: retirement from the sport. No one is immune to the need for rest and recovery.

Recovery And High Performance

Rest and recovery are not luxuries in endurance sports; they are part of the natural training cycle. Doherty et al.'s 2021 study of athletes' sleep and recovery practices states, "Athletes must maintain a balance between stress and recovery and adopt recovery modalities that manage fatigue and enhance recovery and performance in subsequent training/competition."[59]

Endurance athlete coaches regularly prescribe rest as a critical part of training, as the body needs time to repair muscle damage and rebuild taxed immune systems. Not many everyday athletes think they can keep pushing their bodies beyond a certain distance, and few Ironman athletes race injury-free due to repetitive stress.

Athletes understand that sleep is not a bodily chore that must be heeded for the minimal time possible. Instead, they embrace sleep as an essential element of their training. Pro basketball great LeBron James (an endurance athlete, to be sure) often sleeps twelve hours out of every twenty-four, eight to nine hours at night, with a two-to-three-hour nap during the day.[60] Mah et al.'s 2011 study of Stanford University basketball players found that after athletes slept ten hours instead of six hours, they were faster at sprints and had a 9 percent increase in free throw completion percentage.[61] This kind of recovery allows for critical physiological repair and restoration and provides psychological recovery so that athletes continue to perform at their best.

In addition to physical rest, endurance athletes utilize several other strategies to recover from training, such as hydration, nutrition, massage, stretching, and socializing, to name a few. Such strategies seem to have a pretty compelling payoff. Braun-Trocchio et al. (2022) found that "[endurance] Individuals who reported placing in the top three overall in competition used significantly more recovery strategies than those who had not placed in the top three overall for both training…and competition."[62] This study shows that recovery has a direct and positive relationship with athlete performance, and having a variety of recovery strategies further improves performance.

Mental Recovery

One of the most important benefits of such recovery strategies is their impact on *mental health*. For athletes to find a sustainable mental pace, they must unplug now and again to focus on healing their bodies and give their minds a break. In recent years, there has been significant and needed attention on the importance of mental health in professional sports, with several high-profile athletes pulling out of competitions to take care of their mental health.

For example, Kalisha Osaka was fined $15,000 for skipping the news conference at the 2021 French Open. A news article stated, "She framed the matter as a mental health issue, saying that it can create self-doubt to have to answer questions after a loss."[63] US gold medal gymnast Simone Biles dropped out of the 2020 Tokyo Olympics early due to experiencing a significant amount of stress. Afterward, she reflected that she needed to "put myself first, listen to my mind and body, what my heart was telling me to do. I had to put my pride aside and say, 'Okay, this isn't going to work.'"[64] Simone has returned to the sport because of the time spent on her mental health, not despite it.

While most of us will never know the kind of performance pressure professional athletes experience, what is universal is the need to care for ourselves—body, mind, and soul. These athletes show us that the more pressure we feel, the more critical it is to prioritize our mental health to get back in the game and perform at our best.

In my experience with leaders, many think the physical, emotional, and psychological rules don't (or can't) apply to them as they do to endurance athletes. While most leaders will attest to the importance of such strategies—even advocating for them to others in their organizations—most see rest as a luxury. They find it almost impossible to check out for any significant period.

The Business Case For Not Recovering

As goes the old saying, "The definition of insanity is doing the same thing, over and over again, and expecting different results." We know that not recovering from endless work and home stress can lead to poor health outcomes and suboptimize our work and relationship efforts. So why do we continue this insanity? Several factors contribute:

- *A 24-7 work cycle.* Working in a global economy where technology demands round-the-clock attention to our business puts tremendous pressure on companies and leaders to be ever-vigilant to changing needs and demands. We may be required to be on video calls at any hour to ensure we connect with our team, customers, and bosses all over the globe. The drumbeat of need is always there and can be hard to manage.
- *Permeable boundaries between work and nonwork activities.* With the digital revolution came the removal of clear boundaries between work and personal time. Working from home has become a reality

for millions of people. With online messaging forums, chat groups, and AI-assisted messaging production and retrieval, it is continually getting easier for us to connect with work and more challenging to disconnect from it. When was the last time you collapsed into bed, completely exhausted, checking emails until the last second your head hit the pillow? Have you brushed your teeth while tapping out an email on your phone? With fewer natural boundaries between work and nonwork activities, it gets harder and harder for us to put the work down and attend to the rest of our lives.

- *Difficulty managing multiple stressors.* Many of today's managers and leaders find that the number of stressors they face on any given day creates intractable stress. In the American Psychological Association's report of their findings on their 2023 Work in America Survey, they state:

  o "Workplace stress also remains at a concerning level, with 77% of workers having reported experiencing work-related stress in the last month.

  o Further, 57% indicated experiencing negative impacts because of work-related stress sometimes associated with workplace burnout."

  Survey data show that many workers are not getting the breaks from this stress that they both need and want;[65] further, managers are tasked with managing their team's stressors and do not feel they have the tools necessary to do so effectively.

- *Pride/fear/competitiveness.* Managers and leaders are often in their roles because they are take-charge, competitive, and get things done. However, those competitive qualities can also work against leaders as they try to prioritize their wellness. One belief is that pulling away from their work responsibilities for a prolonged period will hurt the business, their team, or their reputation. A contrasting fear is that they will take time away, and the company will continue without them. The latter can be even scarier for many high-achieving people than the former. This can be exacerbated by societal messages telling us that being busy reflects our value to society. But the reality is, if you win at being busier than everyone else, it's likely you lose in other aspects of life. In her book, The Gifts of Imperfection, Brené Brown states, "If we want to live a wholehearted life, we have to become intentional about cultivating sleep and play, and about letting go of exhaustion as a status symbol and productivity as self-worth."[66]

Nowhere are the pressures of work higher than among CEOs. Porter and Nahia's 2018 Harvard Business Review article on time management among CEOs cited that CEOs work 62.5 hours per week on average, while the rest of Americans work 44.8 hours per week on average. And yet, their research shows that CEOs are often closer to professional athletes in their ability to prioritize rest and recovery than many other managers.

Porter and Nohria found, "To sustain the intensity of the job, CEOs need to train—just as elite athletes do. That means allocating time for health, fitness, and rest."[67] Many CEOs understand there must be time for recovery from work tasks, or they will suffer the consequences of prolonged physiological, emotional, or cognitive stress. Just as we saw with some of our famous athletes, prolonged stress can increase the likelihood of developing physical injury or mental health problems, such as anxiety or depression. By taking time to recover mentally and physically, leaders preserve their cognitive and emotional resources for critical resources like decision-making, people leadership, and goal execution.

Work Martyrs Need Not Apply

In Achor and Gielan's 2016 article on taking time off for vacation, they say the case for vacation bears out in promotion rates. As seen below (see Figure 11), people who took ten or fewer vacation days per year were less likely to receive a raise or promotion than those who took more. As the authors say, "Many people have become work martyrs, thinking if they give and give, they will be more successful. But it doesn't play out that way."[68]

Figure 11. The benefits of taking vacation

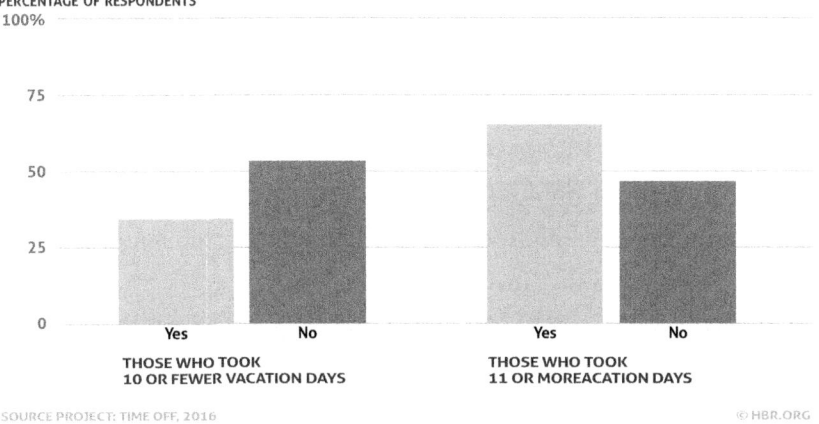

Taking a Vacation Pays Off
If you take at least 11 of your vacation days, you're more likely to receive a raise or bonus.
HAVE YOU HAD A RAISE OR BONUS IN THE LAST THREE YEARS?

PERCENTAGE OF RESPONDENTS
100%

75

50

25

0

Yes	No		Yes	No
THOSE WHO TOOK 10 OR FEWER VACATION DAYS			THOSE WHO TOOK 11 OR MOREACTION DAYS	

SOURCE PROJECT: TIME OFF, 2016 © HBR.ORG

Advocating For Recovery

Do you remember Alex? Alex had outstanding performance in their organization and was considered a high potential. Alex had sacrificed a lot for the company, including moving several times and living through a few years where they barely saw their family.

Over several months, Alex had made it known that they would be less able to travel and take on high-visibility projects due to some family needs. After all their hard work, Alex saw this as a terrific opportunity for some much-needed recovery while still being a vital team member.

Their boss and CEO seemed on board with this plan, so imagine their shock and dismay when one of the senior executives said that Alex would soon be expected to run a high-visibility project in a remote location requiring 50 percent travel for the next twelve to eighteen months. Alex felt this was unfair and a betrayal of their explicit request for time to recover and meet their family's needs. For the first time, Alex—fiercely loyal to the company—considered looking for a position outside the company.

Through our coaching, Alex decided instead to self-advocate and express to their boss and the CEO that Alex felt their needs were being ignored. Bravely, Alex refused to take on the new role. The CEO quickly mobilized, reassuring Alex that the company would find a different role that did not require travel and would still provide high value.

Rather than seeing Alex as not delivering enough, the CEO appreciated Alex asking for what they needed. Alex is now in a role on a special team, reporting directly to the CEO and working with project executives all over the country. This high-visibility, high-impact role could positively influence Alex's eligibility for an executive role.

It took tremendous courage for Alex to advocate and set the boundaries they needed to meet their personal needs. Yet, by taking action, Alex was able to craft a recovery plan that met their needs and provided value to the company.

Reframing FOMO

My colleague Joel Garfinkle, a world-renowned expert on executive presence, has built an incredibly successful consulting and coaching business. Despite being in high demand, Joel takes several consecutive weeks off every year. During that time, he does not respond to work-related calls or emails. He completely disconnects. Joel will tell you that his success is because of this commitment to recovery, not despite it.

For many of us, our FOMO (fear of missing out) is such a powerful force that we could never dream of walking away from our work for an extended period. But Joel chooses to walk directly away from FOMO or perhaps to reframe it. For him, the FOMO might be about fear of missing time with his family, not prioritizing personal relationships, or not giving his brain and body a chance to recover from a rigorous work and travel schedule. Having taken this extended time off annually for over a decade, Joel knows that his business will not only survive but will grow and strengthen.

Recovery can take many forms; what matters is finding a few (or several) ways that work for you. What might work best for you to give yourself the mental and physical edge you need to perform at your best?

- Sleep
- Exercise
- Pursuing hobbies
- Protracted time away from the office/vacation
- Social media moratorium or fast
- Sabbatical
- Thinking time
- Meditation/yoga
- Minibreaks (e.g., Fridays off all summer)
- Social activities
- Scheduled learning time

There are no right or wrong options; the only bad choice is to ignore your recovery needs. Fight magical thinking (the idea that somehow things will get better by hoping they will) by recognizing recovery as critical to your endurance leadership success plan.

Coach's Questions ▬ ▬ ▬ ▬ ▬ ▬ ▬ ▬

- What magical thinking are you engaging in that might keep you from recovering? (For example, "I will take a vacation just as soon as this busy time at work is over," when the reality is the busyness will not end.)

- What FOMO do you have? What other aspects of your life might be neglected due to FOMO?

- What do you love doing that you wish you could do more often? If you could spend 10 percent more time recovering, what difference would that make in your energy, attitude, and physical and mental health? What would you have to do to make that happen?

- What will happen if you do not prioritize recovery?

Training Plan

- List out your critical priorities for the next six months. Is recovery on that list? If not, make it so.

- Articulate the quality, type, and length of recovery you need and revisit it every few months. This may look different every time you do it, as your life needs and wants change. Do you need a protracted vacation or short work breaks in the next six months? Do you recover more with more exercise or more sleep? Plan your recovery schedule according to your needs and wants.

  o Word of caution: going too long without any recovery efforts can create burnout. Ensure you have at least small recovery efforts built into your plan every six to eight weeks.

- Ensure you have an accountability partner for your recovery. This is someone with whom you will share your recovery plan, and they can help you stick to it. Someone who will benefit from you living your plan is a good choice: a partner, family member, or close coworker. Be specific with your plan and find a time to follow up.

- Remember: Recovery is not an excuse to abscond from your responsibilities. You still need to do your job. But recovery can ensure you do it well, with more energy and motivation, and for longer.

PART IV

Forge Discipline

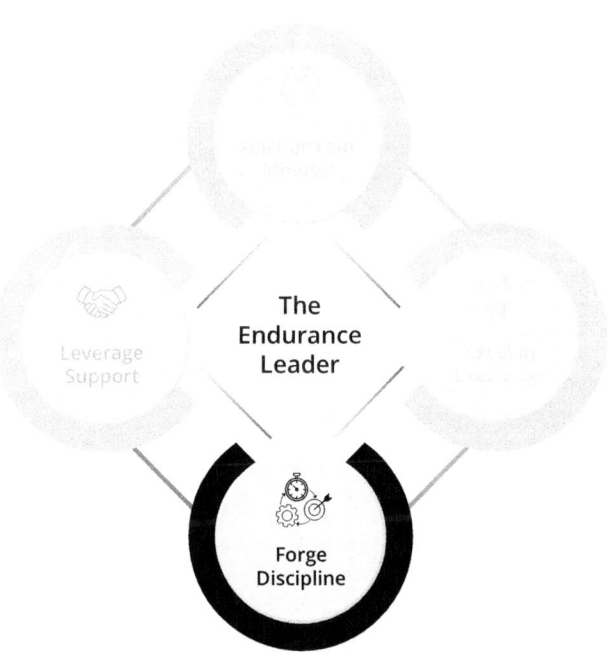

The
Endurance
Leader

Leverage
Support

Forge
Discipline

Chapter 11

Build Mental Toughness

[People say they could never do what I've done.] They start putting all these limitations on themselves, but the hardest thing in any endurance sport is not the physical preparation; it's the mental preparation and the mental toughness.

Scott Rigsby

Toughness Personified

In 2018, Desiree ("Des") Linden became the first American to win the women's division of the Boston Marathon in thirty-three years. While that alone is a fantastic feat, the conditions under which she completed that race were brutal: the temperature was in the high thirties Fahrenheit, it had been raining for a good part of the day, and she and her competitors were facing headwinds up to 25 mph. Despite the conditions, Des accepted the situation and leaned into her mental toughness. Though she never expected to win (in fact, in the beginning, she thought she might drop out), Linden set her mind on the finish line and found a way to escape the negative voices in her head. Part of that toughness was displayed when she stopped partway into the race to wait for her US teammate Shalane

Flanagan, who had stopped to use a portable toilet. By stopping to run with Flanagan, Linden says, "Helping her helped me, and I kinda got my legs back from there."[69]

Linden credits mental toughness with her ability to survive a brutal day and outrun the entire women's field. In a 2019 CNBC interview, she said, "A lot of people will see last year's win, but what they don't realize is that it's thirty years in the making. It was my sixth time running Boston. It takes years to become an 'overnight success,' and it's just showing up day after day and putting in the work."[70]

The Building Blocks Of Mental Toughness

What exactly is mental toughness? Different researchers define it differently; however, the central tenets involve being able to perform well despite adversity:

- "Mental toughness means coping with challenging situations and being focused, motivated, and confident in facing adversity," says Denver-based sports and performance psychologist Haley Perlus, PhD.[71]
- Research by Gucciardi et al. (2015) defines mental toughness as "a personal capacity to produce consistently high levels of subjective (e.g., personal goals or strivings) or objective performance (e.g., sales, race time, GPA) despite everyday challenges and stressors as well as significant adversities … it "can be defined as a state-like psychological resource that is purposeful, flexible, and efficient in nature for the enactment and maintenance of goal-directed pursuits."[72]
- According to research by Yankov, Davenport, and Sherman (2019), mental toughness is evident in some personality elements. They state, "The core of mental toughness is a combination of self-confidence, competitiveness, and emotional control."[73]

These studies suggest that mental toughness combines genetics, environmental factors, and psychological skills training. Using Des Linden as an example, she has some innate ability to push her legs, heart, and mind when running. However, her ability to deliver on her natural gifts depends on how efficient and effective she has become in executing her run form and mental strength in various circumstances. Furthermore, she must have access to environments that do not deplete her energy and mental focus. For example, she cannot expose herself day after day to extreme weather conditions, relentless long runs, or a tyrannical coach, all of which would leave her less than 100 percent when she arrived at the starting line.

Further evidence of the state-like elements of mental toughness is the development of coping skills in adverse situations. In their research, Crust and Clough (2011) found that "Of central importance [to mental toughness] is the development of independent problem-solving and personal responsibility through a challenging yet supportive learning environment. We argue that to develop mental toughness, young athletes must be gradually exposed to, rather than shielded from, demanding situations in training and competition in order to learn how to cope."[74]

For athletes and leaders to remain mentally tough, they need trait-like qualities (e.g., innate confidence and competitiveness) and state-like attributes (e.g., coping skills and emotional control).

Mental Toughness In Personal And People Leadership

Mental toughness exists in endurance leaders as well as athletes. Samir is an endodontist (root canal surgeon) and a military commander. His work involves delicate procedures that require precision measured in hundredths of a millimeter, often on high-ranking officers in the US military. Patients usually come to him in a great deal of pain, and he regularly faces the common phobia that many people have of dental work. On top of it all, Samir's current working environment does not have some of the equipment necessary for him to provide sedation to his patients, which typically stops their pain and anxiety. His only option is to inject them with Novocain, which means they are alert for their procedures.

Samir had a recent patient on whom he was performing a root canal. The patient was terrified and told him that she usually complained when the numbing needle even came close to her. She said she had never had any provider get past that; all previous surgeons had stopped when she got that vocal. As a result, she had not had the treatment she truly needed. Samir and the patient made an agreement that, barring anything drastic, Samir would continue even if she began to complain, knowing that a Novocain injection is not truly very painful.

True to form, the patient began complaining loudly as soon as Samir started getting close to the injection. He soothingly talked with her and began the injection very, very slowly. Despite sounding anxious, she was able to engage him as he led them into a pleasant and unrelated conversation. When he told her he was done with the injection, she was surprised because she hadn't even felt it. After the procedure, the patient said to him that it was the best treatment she'd ever had. She thanked him for their agreement to work through her initial discomfort so that she could receive the treatment. Samir's confidence, steely resilience, and toughness in the face of a stressor most people can't tolerate (loud complaining) allowed him to provide the delicate and complicated treatment needed to get his patient out of pain permanently.

Adding to Samir's mental toughness, he leads a dental clinic with over sixty-five dental professionals and support staff, both military and civilian. A seasoned military leader, Samir could have taken the easy way to leadership when he arrived at his current location several years ago. He could have established a top-down way of engaging with staff and allowed the status quo (which did not consistently address underperformance) to remain unchecked.

Instead, he spent several weeks learning all about the people and their challenges and sharing his leadership philosophy, which is a mix of empathy, forthrightness, and accountability. Some time ago, he had to provide difficult feedback to a longstanding union-represented civilian employee who was not delivering per expectations. No one had provided her honest performance feedback before, and she complained to the union that she was unfairly criticized.

Because this union is powerful, many leaders choose not to engage and allow issues to languish. Rather than turn away from the adversity, Samir leaned into the situation, held his ground, and worked with the union and the employee to ensure clarity of expectations and create a clear path for her success. Months later, she was one of the best performers on the team. By remaining mentally tough during a difficult moment, Samir was able to lead the situation to a favorable outcome for all involved.

It's unlikely that Samir was born with a higher degree of mental toughness than other leaders. However, he desires to continue improving as a leader and a dental provider, which means continuing to challenge himself by embracing difficult circumstances.

Resilience, Grit, And Mental Toughness

The concept of mental toughness can be traced back to early work on hardiness done in the 1930s. Many other terms have been associated with mental toughness, including grit and resilience. What is the difference between these terms? Dr. Brad Cooper does an excellent job differentiating among them, likening them to coping with the past, present, and future.[75] I've paraphrased and embellished his concepts here:

- *Resilience is your response to your past.* It is the ability to overcome difficulties quickly. For example, you may have had a less-than-ideal start to your career, with poor academic performance and perhaps family commitments keeping you from focusing on your occupational growth as much as you would have liked. Your ability to "bounce back" from those adversities and launch a successful career demonstrates a sense of resilience.
- *Grit is future-focused.* It is the ability to remain focused and determined to achieve your long-term goals, even when progress is painfully

slow. In endurance leader parlance, grit is part of staying focused on the finish line, even though it might be miles away.

- *Mental toughness is the present.* It is how you respond to current circumstances; are you willing and able to seek out and cope with demanding situations? This is an active process that allows grit to show up over time. Having resilience and grit may help you activate mental toughness.

Resilience will help you survive, and grit will help you keep the end in mind, but only mental toughness can be built *right now*. You can expose yourself to situations and environments that will push you out of your comfort zone and expand your ability to deliver in challenging circumstances.

Building Mental Toughness

Some mental toughness might be innate (Des Linden's and Samir's confidence and high-performance focus), but some of it can be developed (Des's running efficiency, lung capacity, and mental stamina; Samir's resilience and strong coping skills in a variety of conditions). As endurance leaders, how can we foster the mental toughness to help us thrive in adversity? Here are a few steps you can take to build your mental toughness:

- *Define what mental toughness means to you.* As you look at your long-term goals, what will keep you on the road to your future success? What are the small changes you can make to your daily habits that can help you get closer to your future goals? Perhaps you aim to be more present in your children's daily lives. So mental toughness for you means leaving the office at 6 p.m. three nights per week instead of 7 p.m. That way, when pressure picks up at work, and you are feeling more pressure to work later hours, you will already have built the mental discipline to stay the course and keep your commitments.
  - Part of what will help is *knowing what motivates you.* Return to your ultimate mission; what do you want to achieve in this

lifetime of personal and professional leadership? Remembering that will help you dig into the mentally tough work you might have to engage in to keep the mission alive. In the example above, the motivation is for a "life where my children know me and experience me as a meaningful part of their lives every day."

- *Treat mental toughness like a muscle you want to strengthen.* Do you remember the concept of minimum viable effort? Where can you push your edge and step out of your comfort zone, even to a small degree? Murphy talks about this both in physical and mental terms. Every year, he picks a new physical goal that is a bit harder than last year. And he commits daily to pushing himself a little bit further physically to achieve that goal. He also picks a leadership goal he wants to improve and sets a goal of trying to get better at a tiny aspect of that every week. For example, if he wants to improve as a listener, he might try to slow down his propensity to interject one week and then focus on seeking out new perspectives the next. As James Clear would say, "How can you get 1 percent better every day?" That is how we establish the discipline of mental toughness.

- *Practice being uncomfortable.* It is one thing to survive through discomfort (resilience). It is another thing to seek out places of discomfort. Pursuing discomfort is challenging, particularly when the world feels scary and unpredictable. While we have all heard about the importance of "stepping outside your comfort zone," it can be easier to challenge others than do so ourselves.

Former American Apparel executive and modern-day stoicism advocate Ryan Holiday made a thought-provoking statement on Tim Ferriss's blog: "Comfort is the worst kind of slavery because you're always afraid that something or someone will take it away. But if you cannot just anticipate but *practice* misfortune, then chance loses its ability to disrupt your life."[76] This doesn't mean you have to take an ice-cold shower every day, as Ferriss advocates. But it might mean putting aside your creature comforts or disrupting your current routine to build in time for something you want to achieve. Perhaps it's getting up thirty minutes earlier to exercise and meditate before starting your day. Maybe it's signing up for an improv class to build your public speaking skills. There are multiple ways to approach being uncomfortable. The goal isn't the degree of discomfort; it's finding the edge of what you can tolerate and sustain to achieve your bigger goal.

- *Conquer your don't wannas.* I recall seeing an adult wearing a T-shirt that said, "I cannot adult today." Don't we all want to escape the responsibilities of adulthood occasionally? Some days, we might wish to respond to the demands of life much like a child and say, "I don't wanna!" People practicing mental toughness don't feel that any less than you do; they commit to working through that feeling and doing what they intend to do anyway. Des Linden grew up in Southern California but lives and trains in Michigan. Do you think she faces days when the weather is cold, dark, and dreary? Do you think she might struggle to get out of a warm bed before dawn to train in awful conditions? I bet she does. However, her commitment to mental toughness helped her face her Boston Marathon race-day conditions with endurance.

  As an endurance leader, there will be days when you may feel equally uninterested in pushing yourself. You may feel overwhelmed, busy with other tasks and responsibilities, or stressed by your boss, team, or family's expectations. The way to get through such a don't-wanna moment is to embrace it. Feel it for what it is. It's okay to throw yourself a pity party—just make it the shortest party in the history of parties. Once you feel your anguish, take a few deep breaths. Remind yourself of your strength, your gifts, your capabilities. Then, move on to reminding yourself why you committed to this goal in the first place. What is its significance? What will happen if you do it today, tomorrow, or for your lifetime? What would it mean to do 1 percent of what you committed to? Hopefully, taking the time to acknowledge your feelings will allow you to see them more objectively and reframe your goal of pushing yourself.

- *Surround yourself with people who will support your commitments.* When you want to enhance your mental toughness, look to those who help you remember what you set out to do and challenge you to stick to it. In our current world, we may often feel like things are too hard to push ourselves. And we can seek out those who will validate our excuses. But life doesn't get easier when we go easy on ourselves. To move past your don't wannas, find people who will give you the tough love you need to remember why you set your goals in the first place: friends, colleagues, and family who will push you to achieve your very best because they can see in you what you might not be able to see in yourself at the time. Friends who challenge you to aim high will likely be people pursuing their endurance leadership path. Coaches are also a great resource to help you remain committed to your goal.

The Importance Of Intrinsic Motivation

The human need to compete is deeply rooted in our need for survival. When we sense scarcity, we instinctively compete for resources. This is why people overeat at an all-you-can-eat buffet and crowd the airport gate area to try to board early enough to get a spot for their luggage. The desire to protect our needs can propel us to do things we might otherwise not do. However, for most of us, competition is externally determined. If we do not sense threats or opportunities from the outside environment, we tend to revert to our comfort zone. I work with many organizations that champion continuous improvement programs and even develop competencies that expect leaders to press for more continually. Unfortunately, these efforts are often unsuccessful because they are trying to teach someone to be competitive. Some people don't have the intrinsic motivation to compete unless the circumstances require them to.

To build a mental toughness mindset as an endurance leader, you must revisit your ultimate mission (an intrinsic motivator). Does the mission compel you to do more? Does it evoke a sense of not being settled or satisfied? Murphy's company has seen fantastic growth in his ten years there. We can attribute a good portion of that to his "1 percent better" mindset: "It is the notion of personal commitment, each day to get even just a little bit better. My definition of leadership is my ability to take something from point A to point B."[77] That implies progress and moving forward. When challenges come, Murphy and other endurance leaders do the "next best thing." In other words, you may not be able to do everything, but you can do the next thing to the best of your ability. There's still progress. Note that the difference between Murphy and a company's continuous improvement programs is the locus of motivation. For Murphy, it's internal; the corporate push toward always getting better is external for many leaders.

When we tie our mental toughness to our mission, competition does not have to result in a zero-sum game. It's all about progression. I have observed many triathlon race award ceremonies where a third-place finisher bound happily up to her place on the podium, ecstatic because she exceeded her expectations. She isn't upset she didn't win; she's thrilled that she finished in the top three (I know because I've been that third-place finisher). The same is true for endurance leaders; like Murphy, they take pride in moving things forward daily. They push themselves for the next best thing. Doing so starts with a keen understanding of where you are, where you're going, and what success means to build your long-term objectives.

Mental Toughness In Moderation

While the pursuit of mental toughness can be valuable, there is a cautionary tale to be told about the overapplication of mental toughness. As endurance athletes, countless friends and I have pushed past pain to complete a workout or achieve a race goal. This has resulted in injury that sometimes can take months to heal, if ever. Most of these unfortunate pursuits are due to putting ego and pride ahead of health and longevity. I've seen the same for people who participate in races such as the Tough Mudder or Spartan races, which require things like walking through an electrified wall or crawling through fields of mud. While these activities require toughness, they are not a consistent, day-after-day approach to functional longevity. People may feel tough by completing these, but they might not be doing much for their ability to achieve genuinely higher levels of physical activity.

In the work arena, the same can be true. In a *Harvard Business Review* article, Chamorro-Premuzic and Lusk (2017) describe the downside of overapplied mental toughness at work: "Scientific reviews show that most people waste an enormous amount of time persisting with unrealistic goals, a phenomenon called the 'false hope syndrome.' Even when past behaviors clearly suggest that goals are unlikely to be attained, overconfidence and an unfounded degree of optimism can lead to people wasting energy on pointless tasks."[78] As a consultant and coach, I regularly see leaders trying to push themselves and their teams to goals that may no longer be realistic or attainable. They convince themselves that if they work harder, push everyone for a few more hours, or spend a little more time in meetings, they will get to the goal. The problem is they run the risk of burning themselves out, as well as their teams.

I encourage you to view mental toughness as a tool: Used well, it can help you make substantial gains and achieve goals under adversity. But you must first understand what you are trying to accomplish and why this is the right tool. Used poorly, it can quickly become a weapon that can result in potential injury or suboptimal outcomes for your leadership or team. Ignored altogether, it will not be a ready resource when you most need it to overcome tough times.

Coach's Questions ▬ ▬ ▬ ▬ ▬ ▬ ▬ ▬ ▬

- What will motivate you to pursue mental toughness? What goals might benefit from you pushing outside your comfort zone? What could you accomplish as a leader if you applied more mental toughness this year?

- Who can help you with your mental toughness? What friend/colleague/coach will push you past your excuses to be the person you want to be?

- What can you tell yourself when you just don't wanna? How can you exhibit greater confidence and motivation in the face of adversity?

- If you find yourself pushing yourself or others too hard or feeling like you are banging your head against a wall, reflect. What does this goal mean to you? Are you pursuing it for long-term success or a short-term win? Is it about success or ego? Get the input of a trusted advisor or colleague who can provide a fresh perspective on your potentially overly zealous viewpoint.

Training Plan

- Pick one specific goal on your endurance leadership journey over the next six months. Anticipate the adversity you might face in achieving that goal.

- Develop a strategy for overcoming adversity using mental toughness. Remember the 1 percent rule: where could you push yourself out of your comfort zone to get a little better? For example, your goal is to communicate more effectively in senior-level meetings, but you struggle with public speaking. Perhaps you build your mental toughness by enrolling in a Toastmasters course, taking an improv class, or speaking up in every meeting you attend, even ones where your technical expertise may not be as relevant. Allow silence in meetings you lead. You will build your comfort across various speaking environments by pushing yourself in these ways.

- Track your progress. Develop a scale that will help you recognize you are making progress. In our example, it might be tracking your level of comfort speaking in meetings in general. Rate yourself weekly so you can see how much you are progressing. It is not likely linear, but I guarantee it will be upward.

Chapter 12

Practice Agility

Success today requires the agility and drive to constantly rethink, reinvigorate, react, and reinvent.

BILL GATES

Flexibility When It Matters Most

We learned about Des Linden's remarkable response to horrendous weather conditions with a degree of mental toughness that hurtled her to a Boston Marathon win. While mental toughness helped Linden prepare well for the mental battles she faced on the course, a different quality helped her make some critical decisions before the race started: agility.

While Des had prepared well for the marathon, she and her coach made last-minute decisions to shift her strategy to meet the day's needs. For example, she didn't warm up as usual to conserve warmth and dryness. Instead, she planned to take the first few miles slower, giving her body more time to warm up and acclimate.

This type of last-minute adjustment was possible because Linden had agility. I define agility as thinking, understanding, and responding quickly to changing circumstances to maintain optimal performance. While I define it as an ability, it is built through practice. In Linden's case, she exposed herself to challenging workouts and difficult conditions in the months and years leading up to that race.

Living in Michigan, Linden is used to weather that is often cold and unfavorable to runners and has run in conditions like that fateful April morning in Boston countless times. However, a few years prior, Linden's training involved running on a treadmill at 89 degrees Fahrenheit with 70 percent humidity to prepare for the 2012 Olympics. This training helped Des build mental and physical strength and broad muscle memory, all ingredients for mental toughness. This means that when conditions are less than ideal, her body and mind are ready to perform at superior levels because they know what it takes to succeed. In other words, her mental toughness made her more agile in less-than-ideal conditions.

During the global health crisis mentioned previously, organizations and leaders gained a new appreciation for what it meant to be agile. (Note: This does not refer to Agile Systems, a specific project management strategy. That concept is related to this one but is not pertinent to this discussion.) While organizations were accustomed to living in a VUCA world (volatile, uncertain, complex, and ambiguous), the change to business due to the health issue was unprecedented.

Leaders and organizations had to pivot quickly to protect their workers, stabilize their workflow, and scrape together some positive earnings when their existing playbooks were obsolete. Some did it well while others could not shift their thinking to manage in this unpredictable new world. Exercising those capabilities on demand is difficult when you haven't practiced agility regularly. We saw the downside of the inability to shift, particularly in organizations where people's needs were not prioritized. For example, in 2022, vast numbers of people left their organizations without another job, mainly because they felt their organization or boss didn't care about their well-being.[79]

Removing Our Agility Blinders

Why are we, as leaders, sometimes blind to the importance of agility? Because we are getting satisfactory results. We must be doing great work if our teams perform and move the needle in the right direction. However, we may not get optimal results or lead others to be more effective. Yet, not preparing ourselves for the eventual changes and opportunities that lie ahead can kill our progress and hasten our long-term success. Endurance leaders seek out, consider, and adopt new strategies to push their performance to a higher level. Dissatisfied with solid performance, they embrace the opportunity to embrace the phrase, "Good is the enemy of great."[80]

Nora, whom we met earlier, had been running her organization fixedly for a long time. While she had managers in place to oversee the work of individual employees, she reviewed most of her team's work and intervened, coached, and educated them where needed. In her mind, this model yielded a high degree of success, but her team was not optimized. Her managers could not lead their people because Nora was overinvolved in delegation, work review, and project oversight. She had set up a system that required her to be involved in even minor decisions. She was working long hours, not prioritizing her well-being, and often seemed frazzled in key constituent meetings. But it was success as she knew it.

One of Nora's primary coaching goals was to spend more time in higher-level decision-making to add more strategic value to the company. However, her management strategy interfered with her ability to extract herself from the day-to-day work. Because her department was meeting goals, she did not seem highly motivated to change her behavior initially. She was performing well and wasn't motivated for great.

However, the company's new aggressive growth goals required a shift in how every department conducted its business. This meant changing Nora's team's focus to more interdependent work to better meet client needs. She could no longer be the center point for all work decisions and would have to quickly shift her approach to even meet baseline goals under the new model. While she felt an intense sense of urgency to make these changes, her comfort with maintaining the status quo prevented her from preparing adequately for this shift.

Through our work together, Nora began adjusting her leadership style. She solicited the input of colleagues who excelled at delegation and empowerment. She sought technology experts who introduced her to new software that could automate some of her team's tasks, freeing them up for higher-impact decision-making and project management. She began holding her managers more accountable, which made her face some painful realizations about the caliber of her team and act on performance problems.

Within six months, Nora's organization transformed from the old hierarchical model to a more functional team structure, with (some new) talented managers implementing her strategic direction. They went from solid to high performance through cross-functional and dynamic work, aided by technology platforms that streamlined many day-to-day tasks. As a result, Nora worked fewer hours and on more critical organizational priorities, and the team began to outperform expectations. While there is still work to be done, Nora's eventual commitment to challenge her assumptions about what works best helped her team move from good to great.

While Nora was able to adapt eventually, her initial lack of agility cost her time and energy and negatively affected the organization's success. She had waited until the external world demanded change and, for several months, was unprepared to meet those demands. By contrast, endurance leaders do not wait for external forces to demand change; they monitor themselves and their efficacy regularly and recognize that without challenging themselves, they will stagnate.

Agility In Leadership

For endurance leaders, practicing agility emphasizes soft skills over hard ones. Skills and knowledge-based expertise can be learned. With technological advances, our abilities to succeed functionally may not be based on how much we know but on how much knowledge we can access. What matters is the ability to be flexible in our thinking, the willingness to question our assumptions and admit what we don't know, and the openness to act with humility and curiosity as we try new things.

In 2021, Krupp and Hogan defined leadership agility as "the ability to pivot quickly with an open, flexible mindset to respond rapidly, in real-time, to changing conditions."[81] This competency becomes ever more critical in a world with increasing complexity and uncertainty. They list four key traits that underlie agile leadership:

- *Foresight.* The ability to anticipate the need for change and be ready and willing to pivot while balancing immediate reactions with the long-term impacts of change. Foresight relies on a leader's thinking dexterity, including solving complex problems, thinking logically, and developing effective solutions.
- *Learning.* Agile leaders know what they don't know. They iterate rapidly by trying something, failing, learning, and trying something else to reach an ideal outcome. To be a good learner, leaders must be both curious and humble. In her research on fixed versus growth mindsets, Carol Dweck shows us that a growth mindset can help build the capacity to approach challenges with confidence and self-efficacy. It takes humility to say, "I don't know," and endurance leaders recognize that going it alone will only get them so far. To achieve long-term goals, they seek the opportunity to learn from others.
- *Adaptability.* Beyond shifting their mindset, endurance leaders recognize that the existing models and ways of thinking about problems and answers must be regularly challenged. They challenge their norms and expectations, asking, "What assumptions are we making? What new information exists that might make me/us think differently about this?" This requires assertiveness, self-confidence, personal humility, and social and cultural humility.

- *Resilience.* As discussed earlier, resilience is the ability to bounce back from adversity. It can be challenging to manage setbacks, but with the right degree of self-control, discipline, and focus, plus a positive outlook, endurance leaders can see past the downsides and move forward with confidence and conviction.

These criteria inspire a question: is agility learned or innate? Psychologists like me love to respond to binary questions with yes. Agile leaders possess some underlying traits that may predispose them to act more effectively. Still, those traits will only surface if the leader has the right mindset and behavioral discipline to manifest them. How do we build those elements to strengthen our agility?

- *Make space for agile thinking.* The key to leadership agility starts with embracing it as a critical tool for high performance. Like any tool in your tool kit, you must take it out and use it regularly to keep your usage skills sharp. However, many leaders struggle to make space for agility, especially when days pass fast and furious. Leaders who focus on "sprinting" to their next goal will not prioritize it, assuming they will have what they need for change when needed. That could be likened to preparing for a 5K ocean swim by doing laps in your neighborhood pool. You might be accustomed to swimming the distance, but you will be woefully unprepared for the challenges of waves, currents, heat, sun, and salt (not to mention sea creatures).

    To think with agility, make time to think. Build dedicated time into your weekly schedule to think about your business, your leadership, and what new challenges are emerging. Read about business trends, geopolitical events, and industry analyses, listen to investor calls, or reflect on recent leadership announcements. Posit such questions as:
    - If our business were to have a major shift, where would it be, and how ready would we be to respond and outperform everyone else?

o Where are we too comfortable in our thinking/action?

o What are we not paying attention to? What questions are we not asking ourselves?

o How am I shifting my leadership to meet new demands?

Any of these questions will help you push your thinking into new spaces.

- *Cross-train.* Most successful endurance athletes don't just practice their sport; they cross-train with weights, speed and agility exercises, and even unrelated sports to keep them strong and healthy. They also train under various conditions (à la Des Linden's example) to ensure they are ready for whatever race day throws at them. As an endurance leader, you can build your agility by "cross-training" through several strategies:

  o Spend time in an adjacent part of the business to learn about their challenges or opportunities. It could inform you and your team about how to prepare for what's ahead.

  o Investigate competitors or other industries to learn what they are thinking about/worried about. This can be valuable information about what you should be preparing for.

  o Consult others. Abraham Lincoln regularly sought voices that differed from his own because he believed it was essential to be in the company of people who would challenge his leadership. Like Lincoln, bringing in voices that contrast with your own can help you broaden your perspective and see things you could not otherwise.

  o From time to time, bring in visionaries or big thinkers to challenge the current thinking and help you avoid getting sucked into the comfort of equilibrium and the status quo.

Return To Basics To Build Agility

When you've been doing something well for a long time, you tend to stick with it. Your strategy and output have been successful for some time, so why change now? Leaders and athletes have found the keys to winning and repeatedly deploy the same approach, assuming this leads to optimal results. But what happens when that assumption proves itself vastly incorrect?

A great case study is Tiger Woods's golf career. By 2024, Woods had won eighty-two PGA titles and fifteen major golf championships and had donned the green Masters Champion jacket five times. From outward appearances, since 1997, he has done nothing but win—a picture postcard of an endurance athlete. However, during Woods's career, his game was affected by personal scandals, health issues, and major slumps.

At least five times in the past twenty-six years, Woods dismantled his game and rebuilt his swing.[82] That's an easy decision if you are at the bottom of your game, but Woods was not at the bottom of his game; he was one of the best. But he knew he could be even better. As an endurance athlete who wants to continue to be great, his recent rebuilds have focused on preserving his health. This kind of commitment takes discipline because it requires proactive effort and is not contingent upon having experienced a precipitating problem.

Here are a few strategies that might help you get back to basics and rebuild your leadership game:

- *Question basic assumptions.* Going back to your ultimate mission, review the key assumptions you might be making about how your mission will be achieved. What has changed in the past year? The past five years? How have your strategies for reaching your objectives shifted as a result?
- *Take time away.* Unplugging from your day-to-day environment may help you take a fresh look at your life, leadership, and priorities. Give yourself time to reevaluate your performance-longevity relationship. Are your current leadership practices sustainable? How can you

future-proof your leadership approach and meet future uncertainties with confidence, resilience, and a long-term focus?

- *Use a coach.* A great coach can challenge your assumptions and help you think differently about how you will meet future leadership needs.

We are all born with some degree of agility. However, the best endurance athletes and leaders do not rely on that innate quality to prepare them for the future. They develop agility through intentional effort to be ready for whatever lies ahead. To achieve greatness amid uncertainty, one must plan and practice, get uncomfortable, appreciate, and seek progress, not perfection.

Coach's Questions ▬ ▬ ▬ ▬ ▬ ▬ ▬ ▬

- Where am I naturally the most agile in my leadership? In other words, where am I most likely to challenge myself and step out of my comfort zone? Where am I least likely to do that?

- How do I currently respond to uncertainty and adversity? What strategies or skills can help me respond favorably, embrace change and uncertainty, and grow?

- What do I anticipate will be different in our business a year from now? Five years from now? How will my leadership need to change to ensure we perform at our best?

- What life changes do I anticipate in the next one to three years? How can I start preparing for future success now?

Training Plan

- Schedule time to build your thinking agility. Protect that time as a necessary investment to help you meet future needs. A great way to do that, which doesn't cost any extra time, is to make it part of a regular meeting with a peer or boss.

- Build in leadership cross-training activities, such as spending time with peers, customers, competitors, or critics to discuss future business challenges or learn innovative technologies.

- Link agility activities to your ultimate mission. It will be a lot easier and more motivating to push yourself in new ways if you can see how it can bring you closer to your long-term goals.

- Push yourself and your team to try something new. Expect to fail. Do so fast and use the experience to try another new option.

- Leverage a coach or mentor to help you step outside your comfort zone and strive for leadership excellence.

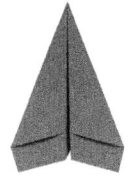

Chapter 13

Plan B—
A Special Kind Of Agility

Agility Versus Contingency Planning

We just learned that agility is the ability to adapt to changing circumstances and still produce high performance. As evidenced by Des Linden, Tiger Woods, and our leader friend Nora, the way to be agile is to plan and practice. For example, you increase your chances of responding well to unforeseen obstacles by looking for new ways of thinking about a challenge, pursuing innovation, or seeking diverse points of view.

Contingency planning is a unique way of understanding agility: it is the intentional preparation of a plan B if plan A doesn't work. It requires focused consideration of multiple futures by uncovering blind spots and dangers that might throw us off course or uncovering opportunities that might compel us to switch up our plan. When plans do not always go as we expect, endurance leaders and athletes have contingencies to help them move forward with greater certainty. Let's look at a few examples from endurance athletes and leadership.

Chris Froome is one of cycling's most outstanding performers of this century. A four-time winner of the Tour de France, Froome is known for his warrior-like qualities, including a 2019 crash that left him in intensive care after a six-hour surgery.[83] During the 2016 Tour de France, while ascending the notorious Mt. Ventoux just a short distance from the day's finish line, Froome and two other riders crashed into a course motorcycle. While the other two riders picked up their bikes and carried on, another motorcycle came up fast and crushed Froome's bike. What would he do? He was wearing the yellow jersey of the Tour's top rider, and there he was, unable to continue. But the legendary cyclist did something completely unexpected: He began running. Up the hill. In his bike shoes. Instead of waiting for help, he moved closer to his goal while help came to him. His support team offered a bike, but it would not work with his shoes, so he rejected it. He eventually swapped bikes with a teammate whose bike was an equivalent size. While he did not win the day, Froome kept his leader status secure, contributing to his Tour de France victory that year.[84]

You may think, "This is a story of agility, not contingency planning." And yes, you are partly right. Froome hadn't planned to run; when he did, people weren't even sure if it was legal, and many posited that Froome would be disqualified. The contingency planning is evident in the bike swap: he and his teammates planned for this kind of what-if scenario. Of course, the more agile you are, the more likely you are to have multiple contingencies. In Froome's case, plan B may have been the bike, but Plan C was getting up that hill in any way possible, which was more accessible due to his incredible physical prowess.

Plan B In Leadership

Endurance leaders also prepare for plan B. Samir, whom you met earlier, oversaw a remote dental facility in a foreign country some years ago. One day, his clinic's water supply was not functioning correctly, and there was a significant risk that the water quality could be compromised. There were patients in the clinic, some in the middle of delicate surgery. Samir immediately deployed clinic staff to work with a nearby grocery store manager to create a supply chain system for bottled water. He also had staff reschedule all nonessential appointments. At the same time, Samir worked with the engineering team at the base to identify and fix the problem. Within forty-five minutes, the clinic had its alternative water supply and a replenishment system. The original problem was resolved within eight hours. Because of his quick thinking and decisiveness, no patients were harmed, and essential treatments were delivered without incident.

Samir and his team were used to contingency planning. They regularly prepared for various challenges due to the nature of their work, the remote location, and the ongoing challenges of serving the American military in a foreign country. They had thought through some of the issues related to water supply, so he already had identified preliminary resources and strategies. While the specifics of this situation (timing, cause, patient impact) were not exactly as they had prepared, Samir's preparation helped his team select options that maximized efficiency while minimizing risk. He had exceptional trust in the judgment and execution capabilities of his team, and he remained agile by leaning into their thinking and decision-making skills to determine the best course of action quickly.

Building A Good Plan B

How do endurance leaders and athletes cultivate and execute an effective Plan B?

- *Planful preparation.* It is not uncommon to see standout athletes move to another sport when either they cannot or do not want to continue in their original activity; think of Michael Jordan (basketball and golf), Michael Phelps (swimming and golf), and Rebecca Romero (rowing and cycling). Each possessed incredible athletic strengths and instincts but also spent time building their physical endurance by cross-training. That versatility made it easier for them to transition from one sport to another. They had a plan B waiting for them when they were ready to retire from plan A.

  Endurance leaders also demonstrate exceptional versatility by consistently seeking ways to broaden and strengthen their skills. For example, they take an active role in learning the business, not just within their areas of technical expertise or the parts that directly affect them. They use mentors from other disciplines or industries to help them open their aperture and see new possibilities or threats. They engage in reverse mentoring with junior team members to gain insights on innovative technologies or modern communication strategies or identify emerging human resource needs. They put themselves in new situations and environments to test their capabilities and learn from failure. These agility-increasing strategies help leaders do a better job of preparing for Plan B.

• *The discipline to push through adversity.* Part of what allowed Chris Froome to run successfully up the climb was his incredible physical prowess. Froome is no stranger to discipline: his many hours of suffering through grueling physical training and a military-like commitment to adequate sleep and optimal nutrition help him maintain his mental and physical strength in the face of adversity.[85] His discipline ensures that when the need for plan B happens, his body and mind are ready and able to make the shift.

Endurance leaders understand the importance of discipline in helping them through unexpected changes. Agility exercises and contingency planning take time and effort, which can be difficult if you feel constantly compelled by what author Charles Hummel described as "The Tyranny of the Urgent."[86] Readying yourself and your team for unpredictability requires focus, patience, and tenacity. Without taking adequate time to consider challenges and opportunities, you may be called to employ a plan B you know little about, reducing your levels of certainty and potentially reducing your performance and impact.

• *Distinguishing between unpredictability and uncertainty.* Research shows that there is a difference between unpredictability and uncertainty. Unpredictability is environmentally driven and changes depending on factors outside of your control.[87] Things become more predictable when they begin to follow set patterns. Uncertainty, however, is internally constructed: it is our degree of confidence that, for example, our actions will lead to desired outcomes. This has everything to do with our knowledge, experience, and support, as well as our fears, anxieties, and self-confidence. Contingency planning will not increase the predictability of what happens (who could have predicted that bizarre bike-wrecking crash in the Tour de France?). Still, it can increase the certainty that there can be a solution to move us toward our objective (crashes are common in the Tour), and therefore, we can have a good backup plan for when one happens.

- *An ownership mindset.* Froome would not have been blamed if he had had a temper tantrum on the course at that moment—after all, what had just happened to him was not his fault. Instead, he realized that he and he alone had the keys to turn this disaster around to success. Rather than dwelling on what happened, he focused on what was still possible. He did not have time to ponder, complain, or sulk—seconds meant everything. He took charge of his situation and made the best possible decision for his and his team's success.

When work efforts do not go well, endurance leaders also take ownership and agency. Instead of focusing on what they cannot do, they act with what they can do. As Murphy said earlier, they do the "next best thing."

For example, Maureen was the CEO of a light manufacturing company. She made a case to her board for an acquisition (plan A). A few on the board dissented, feeling it was the wrong business opportunity. Instead of becoming frustrated, Maureen listened to the concerns and returned to the crux of the opportunity: a chance to bring in recent technology to help them grow their product line (plan B). She worked with her team to source new opportunities that would still meet the overall objective. A different acquisition opportunity emerged within a few months, which the company took. That acquisition added 30 percent to their revenues in the first year. Maureen did not blame the board for the missed opportunity of plan A. She did not get frustrated with her team. Instead, she utilized what she knew was important to the board at its core to introduce a successful alternative.

- *Decisiveness.* Froome knew he did not have time to wait—every millisecond was eating away at his Tour de France yellow jersey leader status. While running was an unconventional strategy (and foolhardy to some), each footstep was one step closer to his goal. As he reflected after the race, "That day, obviously, I didn't want to lose, and it seemed logical in my mind to keep moving forward, even if it meant running."[88]

  When plan A doesn't work, there is often little time to move to plan B. Endurance leaders recognize that and do what they can to gather as much data as possible to make a reasonable assessment, weigh their options, and employ some version of plan B. It may not be perfect, but it will get them closer to their goal. While decisiveness is often considered innate, it can be built with discipline and focus. Decisive leaders can help reduce uncertainty through proper preparation and picking a good plan B in the first place. When things aren't working, they encourage their team members to speak up and listen to their ideas to look broadly at the best possible next steps. They exhibit a high degree of confidence and a willingness to be wrong, make mistakes, and even fail. They recognize that moving forward, however not pretty it may be, is better than remaining stuck in a solution that no longer works.

We all have tales of when our best-laid plans have failed. If you look closely, you will see that your most effective responses have been when you were ready with a good enough alternative (there is no perfect plan B—

otherwise, it would be your plan A!) and the confidence and conviction to move one step closer to your goal.

Coach's Questions ▬ ▬ ▬ ▬ ▬ ▬ ▬ ▬ ▬

- Looking forward over the next six months, where are your business's two to three most significant challenges or uncertainties? What plans do you already have in place to address those? What are your contingency plans if your immediate plans don't work out? Could you reduce the uncertainty of an undesirable outcome by spending more time preparing with your team?

- Ask yourself those same questions on a personal level. How can you build greater confidence and reduce uncertainty in the face of some personal unknowns?

- How disciplined are you about contingency planning for significant events or new needs? How can you build greater discipline to future-proof your business decisions (e.g., preserving time for contingency planning, spending more energy and effort in future planning with colleagues and team members)?

- When things don't go as planned, how do you typically react? What can you do to exhibit greater confidence, poise, and decisiveness in those moments so you can move forward with a good enough plan B?

Training Plan

- Build contingency planning time into discussions on high-impact, high-risk problems. In regular discussions with your team, consider these questions:

  - What could get in the way of our success?

  - What has changed since we first put our solution together?

  - If our solution isn't producing success, what might be our next best option? What strategies/resources/people do we need to employ our plan B?

  - How can we help each other reduce uncertainty even when things are unpredictable?

- Ensure you meet unplanned events with a mindset of ownership and decisiveness. Remain calm when things don't go as planned. Reframe the situation and protect against catastrophizing or withdrawal. Use this as an opportunity to lean into learning and demonstrate agility. Seek the counsel of others. Collaborate with your team. Take ownership and remember that progress is still progress, no matter how slow.

Chapter 14

Learn From The Epic Fail

━━ ━━ ━━ ━━ ━━ ━━ ━━ ━━ ━━ ━━ ━━ ━━ ━━ ━━ ━━ ━━ ━━

You might never fail on the scale I did, but some failure in life is inevitable. It is impossible to live without failing at something unless you live so cautiously that you might as well not have lived at all—in which case, you fail by default.

J.K. Rowling

Is Failure Necessary For Success?

Failure. What thoughts, emotions, and physical reactions immediately rise to the surface just reading the word? Few words conjure up so much visceral response. Failure is human nature, yet most of us do our best to avoid it. After all, we are all striving for success, not failure. But what if instead of thinking of failure as the opposite of success, we saw it as a necessary path on the way to success?

Michael Jordan has often been viewed as the epitome of an endurance athlete. He played fifteen seasons of professional basketball, three of professional baseball, was a gold medalist for the US Olympic basketball team, and much more. But he had more than his share of failures along the way. Jordan was cut from his high-school varsity basketball team because his

145

coach felt he wasn't tall enough (only 5'10" at the time). Jordan considers that failure, along with many more, critical to his future success. Jordan's thoughts on failure were captured in a 1997 Nike ad: "I have missed more than nine thousand shots in my career. I have lost almost three hundred games. Twenty-six times, I have been trusted to take the game-winning shot and missed. I have failed over and over and over again in my life. And that is why I succeed."[89]

While the quote is inspirational, it assumes that somehow failing will create success, which we know falls into our magical thinking category. Failure does not create success. Instead, the willingness to take risks to fail and learn from experience can make us better and *lead* to success. While perhaps not as famously known, some other quotes by Jordan are far more reflective of his relationship with failure:

- "I can accept failure; everyone fails at something. But I can't accept not trying."
- "My attitude is that if you push me towards something that you think is a weakness, then I will turn that perceived weakness into a strength."
- "If you're trying to achieve, there will be roadblocks. I've had them; everybody has had them. But obstacles don't have to stop you. If you run into a wall, don't turn around and give up. Figure out how to climb it, go through it, or work around it."[90]

What differentiates Jordan's approach from most of us is that he did not simply accept failure; he sought it out and learned from it. He sees failure as something to embrace rather than avoid or endure.

Looking Failure In The Face

Failure can teach valuable lessons that endurance leaders use to make them better. For example, I worked with a coaching client, Ilaria, some years ago. Ilaria was a brilliant physician working in research and development (R&D) for a specific product line at a global biopharma company for years. She was so talented that her leadership decided to promote her to the medical director of the product line. While they thought this was a wonderful thing, Ilaria was miserable. She did not have the knack for managing a diverse array of people; no matter what she tried, she felt it wasn't working. Our goal in coaching was to help her build critical management skills, but we weren't achieving sustained success. Ilaria felt like she was failing every day (and I felt like I was failing as a coach). The day I knew we were at the epic fail was the day she said, "You know what, Ann? All I want to do is stay home all day and pet the cat."

You might feel Ilaria didn't fail per se. She accepted a promotion (a good thing) and realized too late that it wasn't a good fit. But it was an epic fail to her, and that is what mattered. At that moment, we had to step back and recognize that our coaching approach was not working and wasn't going to, no matter how hard we tried. Instead, we had to determine how to learn from this experience to help Ilaria get to a better place. I encouraged her to be honest with her boss, saying she wanted to work with products and other technical people who could help grow the product line, not in a general management role. We discussed some plan B alternative roles that she might be able to pitch to him that would be a better fit for her and still allow her to have more responsibility. She spoke to her boss, and they crafted a role within R&D, specifically trading upon Ilaria's strength to bring new insights into the product line. Recognizing the failure of her lack of fit in a broad management role led to a resounding success that may not have been possible without that failure.

The F-Word (Failure)

It took Ilaria and I a long time to admit we were failing. Why is it so hard to accept the F-word (failure)?

- *Our brains are more responsive to success than failure.* Many studies show that when we succeed, our brains emit several positive neurotransmitters, such as endorphins, dopamine, and serotonin.

When failure has a negative consequence, the brain activates the fight-flight-freeze response. It releases cortisol, the body's primary stress hormone, to help us manage fear and regulate our emotions. However, research by Histed et al.[91] found that if there is no immediate consequence to a failure, there may not be much change in brain activity. In other words, we associate success with positive mental and affective states, while failure is associated with neutral or unproductive conditions. Like Ilaria, we may tolerate failure rather than feel a strong sense of urgency to do something about it.

- *Failure has social costs.* Despite much talk of embracing failure in the past several years, most Western acculturated people and organizations have a single mindset around this topic: "Failure is not an option." Our work environments are not spaces where smart failure[92] is accepted, and failure is associated with significant threats. I've worked with countless leaders who've developed an unrealistic but pervasive belief that a single failure will cost them their jobs. This inevitably leads to risk avoidance to head failure off at the pass. Or, when failure does occur, people resort to unhealthy thinking and behavior such as guilt or shame, finger-pointing, judgment, and harsh scrutiny. Despite the disastrous implications of an unwillingness to embrace failure, leaders in organizations continue to promulgate cultures where failure is regularly avoided. (The Harvard Business School case study on NASA's Challenger disaster is a fitting example where consideration of failure was repeatedly silenced, to disastrous effect.[93])

- *Equilibrium and inertia are powerful motivators.* Whenever we try something different, we are subject to internal and external forces that want to pull us back to the familiar. Inertia dictates that objects at rest remain at rest—unless force is applied. As people with constantly busy, pressured lives, inertia may be less of a choice than a de facto position. We may tell ourselves, "I just don't have time to try something new." Similarly, our work environments can exacerbate inertia through the pressure to maintain equilibrium. Humans like predictability. As a group, we excel at subtly or directly discouraging others from trying new things with statements like, "It will never work," "We tried that years ago," and "When it blows up in your face, don't come crying to me." Such responses aren't very inspirational or encouraging of change. So, between our self-talk and the chatter from others, it can be challenging to find the energy, motivation, and support that is often needed to try something new, let alone embrace and learn from failure.

Failure—A Fascinating Continuum

Not all people avoid accepting failure. Benjamin Zander is the conductor of the Boston Philharmonic Orchestra, an organization he founded almost fifty years ago. His willingness to help people embrace failure as a learning opportunity is among his endearing qualities. A clip from a 2008 PopTech video shows Zander sitting with a fifteen-year-old cellist, Nikolai, discussing the performance Nikolai had just finished. He calls to mind an error Nikolai made in the piece and observes that Nikolai's countenance shifted at that moment: Nicolai winced, and his body drew inward (reminding us of the fight-flight-freeze response and the immediate release of cortisol). The next time Nikolai makes an error, Zander recommends that Nikolai should raise his arms above his head and shout, "How fascinating!" which Zander immediately demonstrates, to the delight of the entire audience. He talks about how difficult this is, but the importance of opening oneself to what is possible when a mistake opens the pathway to learning.[94] Carol Dweck's work on growth mindset applies again: if we are open and humble enough to receive what the moment gives us, we can further our pursuit of greatness.

In her 2011 *Harvard Business Review* article on failure, Amy Edmondson admonishes the current organizational approach to failure. She challenges two core beliefs: (1) that failure is always bad and (2) that learning from it is always straightforward.[95] She believes that when leaders think of failure as nonbinary, it removes the idea that a human (or group of humans) must always be to blame for it. Edmondson's approach (see Figure 12) shows failure as a continuum that falls into three major nodes: preventable, complexity-related, and intelligent. This can be difficult in organizations that pride themselves on accountability because it takes a more complex and nuanced approach to thinking about failure. Particularly as we navigate a world that is increasingly complex and uncertain, we may find that many of our organizational missteps are less about "deviance" (which is present in only 3 to 5 percent of failures) and more about inadequate processes or not knowing how to deal with what we don't know.

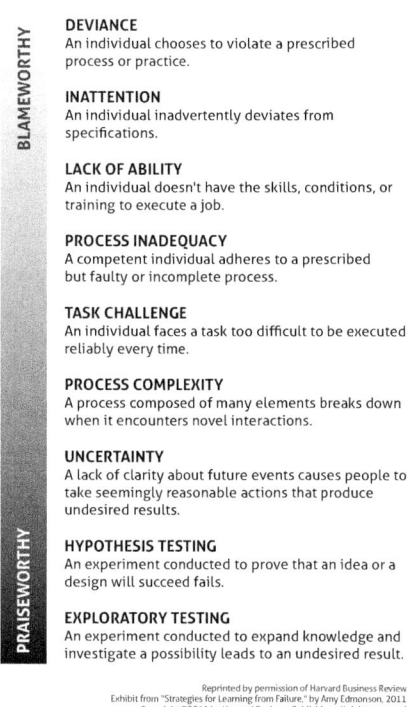

DEVIANCE
An individual chooses to violate a prescribed process or practice.

INATTENTION
An individual inadvertently deviates from specifications.

LACK OF ABILITY
An individual doesn't have the skills, conditions, or training to execute a job.

PROCESS INADEQUACY
A competent individual adheres to a prescribed but faulty or incomplete process.

TASK CHALLENGE
An individual faces a task too difficult to be executed reliably every time.

PROCESS COMPLEXITY
A process composed of many elements breaks down when it encounters novel interactions.

UNCERTAINTY
A lack of clarity about future events causes people to take seemingly reasonable actions that produce undesired results.

HYPOTHESIS TESTING
An experiment conducted to prove that an idea or a design will succeed fails.

EXPLORATORY TESTING
An experiment conducted to expand knowledge and investigate a possibility leads to an undesired result.

BLAMEWORTHY

PRAISEWORTHY

Figure 12. Amy Edmonson's Failure Continuum

Let's apply this to the endurance leader. In a business environment with constant pressure to expand and improve, we must be willing to look outside our comfort zone for fresh solutions. We need to leverage a growth mindset to experiment and allow for smart failure (i.e., not fail the same way twice). When we inevitably fail, we need to avoid the knee-jerk reaction of blaming ourselves or others. Instead, if we can apply Edmondson's spectrum, we might find that the reason for failure lands somewhere on the continuum outside of the blame game.

The Dangers Of Toxic Positivity

The self-help movement has helped people nurture themselves and grow in countless ways. Over the past few years, however, it has seen a disturbing rise in the peddling of toxic positivity. Toxic positivity is an absence of empathy that is sugarcoated with platitudes that have little to do with supporting the recipient. Whitney Goodman, who authored a book on toxic positivity, says, "At its core, toxic positivity is a form of gaslighting. It tells people that what they're feeling isn't real, they're making it up, and that they're the only one who feels this way."[96]

What does toxic positivity sound like? Let's say you've made a disastrous error at work. Your colleague comes up to you shortly after that and says, "It's no big deal; you will do better next time," and walks away rather than helping you process the error to help you learn from it. While the sentiment may seem well-intended, it conveys that spending energy on evaluating failure and extracting its best learning lessons isn't worthwhile. This has many of the same drawbacks as saying, "Failure is not an option." Toxic positivity drives the real conversation about failure underground (or avoided altogether), minimizing its ability to provide learning opportunities and organizational or leadership value.

The other problem with toxic positivity is that it makes people feel worse, particularly when they fail. McGuirk et al.'s 2018 study found that "the overpromotion of happiness, and, in turn, the felt social pressure not to experience negative emotional states, has implications for maladaptive responses to negative emotional experiences."[97] When people experience toxic positivity in response to their failure, it stifles learning, reduces psychological safety, and increases risk avoidance. When facing failure, great leaders search for meaning, not platitudes. They evaluate smartly and use that knowledge and experience to make adjustments that will better position them in the future.

Endurance leaders push themselves and their teams enough that some failure is inevitable. What is essential is how that failure is managed. Do we pause to gather feedback and learn from our mistakes? Do we see failure on a continuum and understand its context and implications for our work? Do we respond to errors with toxic positivity, which doesn't allow people to feel heard, or do we invoke empathy and understanding, creating the space and opportunity to learn? How we approach the epic fail can be crucial to how well we perform in the long term.

Coach's Questions ▬ ▬ ▬ ▬ ▬ ▬ ▬ ▬ ▬ ▬

- What reactions do you have to the word failure? What would building a more positive relationship with the term/idea take?

- What's the biggest failure you've had at work/life? What was the biggest downside to that failure? What was its most significant benefit? Would you have gotten that benefit without that failure?

- What was your most recent failure? Using Amy Edmondson's failure continuum, where is that failure? Do you understand it differently, viewing it through that lens?

- Where might you be holding yourself back because of a fear of failure?

- How can a growth mindset help you mitigate any fears or worries associated with failure?

Training Plan

- Write down your last big failure. Stand up, put your arms in the air, and say, "How fascinating!" (Go ahead, I'm watching.)

- Write down why that failure is fascinating. What did you learn from it? How has it made you better?

- Name one or two things you'd like to try but are afraid you might fail. Write down the factors that might lead you to fail and the likelihood (in percentages) of those happening. Lastly, write down the potential consequences of failure and the potential likelihood of each of those.

I want to try...	What might cause it to fail?	How likely is it to fail (%)?	Consequences for failure	How likely are the consequences (%)?	Risk mitigation strategy

- Now that you've objectively considered the likelihood of failure, how likely are you to try those things? How could you mitigate the risk of failure? Could you invoke the MVE concept to reduce risk by even 1 percent?
- Determine who can help you process and learn from your next failure. How can you make it a smart failure?
- Create a reframe/mantra to help you manage failure. What language can keep you focused on learning (without dipping into toxic positivity)?
- Lastly, plan a risk mitigation strategy. That might be a Plan B, or it might be a mental toolkit to help you remain positive and future-focused in the face of failure. Make a commitment and give it a try!

PART V

Leverage Support

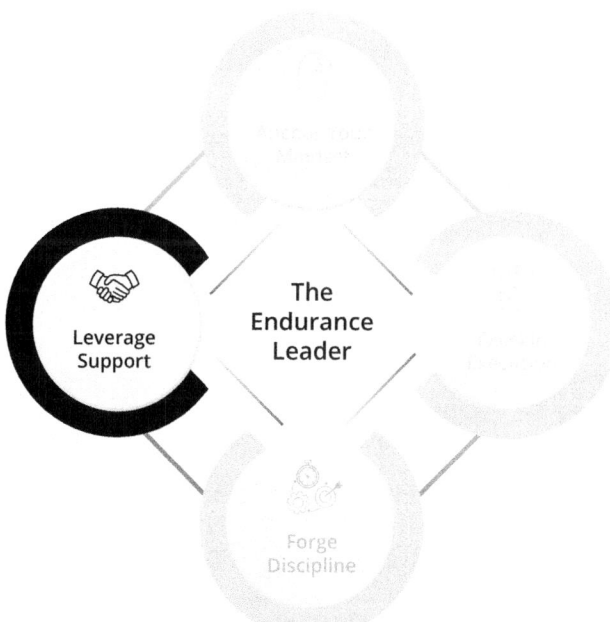

The
Endurance
Leader

Leverage
Support

Forge
Discipline

Chapter 15

Get The Right Coach

A good coach can change a game.
A great coach can change a life.
JOHN WOODEN

The Risks Of Going It Alone

Some time ago, I met a young man in his late twenties, the friend of a young woman whose parents are my neighbors. He was training for an Ironman race in Lake Placid, NY. As an Ironman finisher, I was curious about his training and readiness for the race, as it was only eight weeks away. He struggled to answer most of my questions because he'd spent little time learning about the race. While he'd never attempted an endurance event of this distance, he didn't feel he needed a coach. A former collegiate swimmer and US National Team rower, he thought he had the strength and mindset to carry him through the rigorous preparation required for this kind of race. He did not see the value in a coach or a virtual coaching plan. I wished him well.

When I saw the girl's parents some weeks later, I asked about the young man and his training. They said, "We're not allowed to talk about it." He was no longer going to compete in the race. His training had fallen entirely off; he'd been doing little swimming, biking, or running to prepare, and he was not going to be ready for the incredible feat of endurance required to complete the race. It was such a sore subject that people had to tiptoe around him.

While I may never know what happened to his training, I hypothesize that his decision to go it alone and not use a coach factored into his decision. Similarly, I've met many leaders who have bypassed coaching in pursuing leadership excellence. Many remind me of this young man: excellent background, strong technical skills, and supreme confidence. However, they don't know what they don't know, so they cannot benefit from those who can see around corners they've not yet faced. They may lack some of the discipline that coaches demand. They tend to neglect self-reflection and insights that can help them (and their coach) identify problems and address them before they become ingrained. They also don't have the emotional and psychological support that a coach can provide when the going gets tough.

Many of these leaders have had remarkable success, particularly in the short term. However, as pressures and complexities increase, sustaining energy and adjusting to the increasing demands of leadership becomes more difficult. Some leaders burn out, give up, and stop trying to make positive change. Others allow bad habits to go unchecked, affecting followership. Like uncoached endurance athletes, effort and ego can only take you so far. When your natural gifts are no longer enough, and you need to keep going, the value of a coach is most apparent.

Coaching As Key To Performance

We cannot even fathom a professional-level athlete trying to make it in high-stakes environments without at least one coach. If you sign on to a National Football League (NFL) team, you are likely to have not one coach but up to six, depending on your position. It is because coaches have the abilities and insights to help you make improvements you could not achieve independently. When an athlete we know or admire has a coach, we don't question why that would be a good idea because it is understood that coaches help people achieve higher performance levels. Why would we expect less focus on coaching in the leadership space?

The World Triathlon Corporation, owner of the Ironman races, states that 40 percent of the athletes competing in Ironman or half-Ironman races will either hire a coach or purchase a training plan devised by a coach.[98] What if 40 percent of the leaders you know used a coach? Do you think they would lead differently? How would those changes affect you?

I have a saying about psychotherapy that applies equally well to coaching: "I've never met someone who couldn't benefit from coaching. They may exist, but I haven't met them yet." Many people believe they can get through leadership (and life) without the support a formal, trained professional can provide. But do you want to survive leadership, or would you prefer to lead at your best? Do you believe there might be an expert who could help you lead well across your life? If so, you might consider a coach as part of your endurance leader support team.

If you are considering using a leadership coach, it's worth delving into what constitutes the right coach for you and what you should do to prepare for the coaching journey.

Coaching Trial—And Error

According to the International Coaching Federation 2020 report on the state of coaching, there were an estimated 71,000 coach practitioners in the world in 2019 (i.e., not leaders or managers who use coaching skills, but people explicitly trained as coaches). This figure is 33 percent higher than it was in 2015.[99] With all these coaches, it can be hard to determine the right person to support you on your endurance leadership journey. It might be tempting to select someone local with solid business acumen and an excellent reputation. But just like a personal coach for endurance athletes, other factors must be considered, such as your coaching goals, the coach's style, and the chemistry between the two of you. I will share a personal story that shows how wrong it can go when those factors aren't aligned.

Several years ago, I moved to Florida. I was almost fully recovered from a violent hip break due to a biking accident the year before and was excited to relaunch my endurance athlete career. I began looking for a triathlon coach who could understand my injuries and help me design an intelligent plan for returning to the sport. I found a local coach, Kathleen, through an online search. On an introductory call, I told her about my previous injury and that I was currently recovering from stress fractures in two of my toes. She acknowledged my concerns but didn't seem to pay much mind.

Kathleen and I met for the first time at a track so she could get some measures of my baseline fitness. She had me run three one-mile runs at my maximum speed. Given what I'd told her about my feet, I thought that was ridiculous, but I am compliant, so I did it. I had some of the fastest times I've ever run, but my toes weren't happy. My ability to produce those times kept me engaged with Kathleen, thinking that working with her would make me faster and better. I continued the coaching engagement despite a nagging voice in my head that questioned if she was looking out for my best interest.

I made significant strides in my training over the next few months of our work together but at a cost. I credit Kathleen for providing me with challenging workouts and supporting me by being present for several of them. However, Kathleen wanted to become a nationally recognized coach. That meant she invested most of her coaching time and energy in younger athletes with much more talent. These prodigies were more likely to earn podium spots (finishing in the top three in their age group) at regional and even national races, which would spotlight her coaching. I knew this because when we had group practices with all of Kathleen's coachees, she would design the workouts for them and spend time with them almost exclusively. I would try to keep up, but often, the sessions were too difficult or too risky for my injuries. My injuries were getting worse, not better. After about three months, I realized I needed to stop working with Kathleen. I was not getting much of her time (although I was paying her handsomely), and she wasn't attending to my unique needs enough to recognize the risks in my training program. I wanted a coach who would prioritize my health and longevity; she wanted a coachee who was fast and capable of winning.

I learned the hard way that just because your coach is skilled and knowledgeable, it does not make them the right fit for your needs. While there are some qualities that all good coaches share, there are also stylistic elements that you must ensure are a good fit for your needs and goals.

The Makings Of A Great Coach

To avoid making the kinds of mistakes I made, it is helpful to understand the types of coach characteristics you should look for. Kavussanu et al. (2008) showed that coaches provide several benefits to athletes: they develop the athlete's mental, physical, technical, and tactical abilities; moreover, they help the athlete win.[100] Below is a list of the qualities and actions often attributed to good athlete coaches:

- Committed, disciplined, and organized
- Provide an athlete-centered relationship
- Hold athletes accountable
- Build a relationship of trust, confidence, and respect
- Provide well-planned, highly structured, and realistic practice environments
- Demanding for the sole purpose of making the athlete better
- Ability to read, analyze, and evaluate athlete potential

Endurance leaders also value many of these same qualities in their coaches. Boysen (2019) described qualities like those found by Kavussanu et al. that led to effective coaching interventions. She found that a strong connection and relationship is a hallmark of a trusted, productive, and professional coaching relationship.[101]

As you consider using a coach, consider what elements of this relationship are negotiable and which are less so. Don't compromise on the most important things. At the same time, be willing to consider coaches with an approach that differs from yours enough to keep you engaged, challenged, and supported.

What Works For You?

With so many coaches in the world, there are almost as many different coaching styles as there are coaches. In their 2019 Harvard Business Review article on leaders acting as coaches, Ibarra and Scoular[102] provide a broad framework for thinking about coaching styles (see Figure 13). In their view, the best coaching style depends on the coachee's needs.

Figure 13. Styles Of Coaching

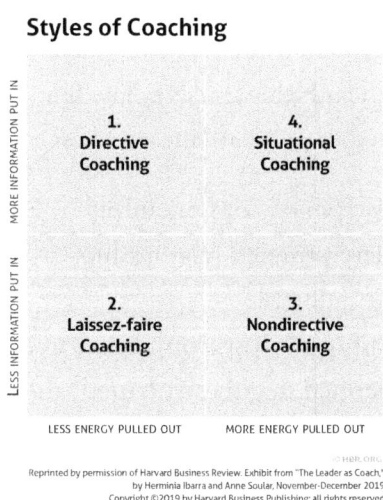

Styles of Coaching

To understand the model:

- The Directive coaching quadrant is associated with telling. This is where mentoring and advising fall. It provides the specifics of how to solve problems but doesn't unleash much motivation in the coachee.

- In the Laissez-faire quadrant, we find coaches who generally leave people alone. This can be effective when a person is being productive, and coaching isn't going to help much.
- In the Nondirective quadrant, a coach generally extracts ideas from the coachee through listening, asking questions, and withholding advice or judgment. This can be useful for many coachees but does not allow for the guidance and direction seasoned leaders often seek.
- Situational coaching allows for both directive and nondirective styles, which captures the best of both worlds of advising and soliciting creativity and input from the coachee/leader.

While most professional leadership coaches are facile across all quadrants, knowing if you need more of one style than another might help you consider which coach will best fit your goals.

Coaches range widely in terms of their characteristics. For example, some coaches are psychologists or therapists who leverage deep theoretical foundations in psychology. Others are seasoned business executives who rely on their experience and business insights to coach. Others may not have either of those backgrounds but have earned a professional coaching certification that informs their practice. Still others are self-trained and use intuitive skills.

A coach might be quiet or loud, analytical or practical, funny or serious, tough or easygoing. There are coaches from every racial demographic, gender, ethnicity, religion, sexual orientation, and type of ability. Some coaches are athletes, knitters, artists, yogis, or gamers. Those hobbies and interests may affect the way they coach. The reality is that most coaches are some combination of several of these disciplines, experiences, interests, and styles. Understanding what the coach brings to the coaching relationship will be critical to determining who is the right fit for you and helping you build a successful working relationship.

If you want to leverage a coach to help you become more of an endurance leader, ask prospective coaches the questions in the table below (see Figure 14). Two words of caution: (1) ensure you know your range of acceptable answers before you ask, and (2) do not try to ask them all. Select a few that are most important to you.

Figure 14. Prospective Coach Questions

How long have you been coaching? What are your credentials for the work?
How does your background inform your skills and style as a coach?
What philosophies/frameworks do you use in coaching?
What is the typical demographic of your client base? (This question can be about leadership level, but it might also be about industry, racial composition, gender, or other factors that are meaningful to you.)
Why did you begin coaching?
How do you measure success in coaching? What are some outcomes we might expect?
How do you measure progress in coaching? What happens if we aren't making progress?
What's important to you in a coaching relationship?
What will working with you provide me that I cannot get from another coach or mentor?
How do you like to provide feedback? What is your style when you want to push or challenge your clients?
What do you value, and how does that show up in your coaching work?
How do you handle confidentiality? *

How do we determine when a coaching engagement should end?
What was your worst coaching engagement, and what did you contribute to that? What did you learn from that experience?
If I talked to three of your recent coaching clients, what would they tell me they liked most about working with you? Liked least?

*Confidentiality is complex when a company pays for a leader's coaching. The boundaries should be clearly defined before coaching begins.

Are You Ready For A Coach?

While coaching can be an excellent resource for every leader, not every leader is ready for a coach. An excellent coaching engagement starts with a leader with the right motivation, insight, attitude, and discipline to make the effort worthwhile.

Allow me to illustrate two different cases in readiness. I participate in the Coaches' Gift program, run by my talented and lovely colleague Val Markos. The program provides four months of coaching, free of charge, to vetted nonprofit leaders. David, whom we met earlier, was my first leader in this program. When I read David's application for the program, I knew he was motivated. Everything about his description of himself, goals for coaching, insights into his strengths and development areas, and extreme ownership over his improvement told me he was ready to leverage coaching to take him to the next level in his leadership.

Working with David is the manifestation of that motivation. David is on fire whenever we meet: eager to share, learn, and be challenged. He does his homework between sessions and comes ready to discuss his learning. He is keen to get feedback from his team about his growth areas. He takes accountability and gives appreciation to those who hold him accountable. David listens intently, takes notes, and uses our discussions in real-life situations. He is humble, appreciative, and curious. Working with David for those first four months was such a joy that I am still working with him pro bono two years later.

By contrast, I started pursuing an opportunity with another leader in the program, Violet. In our initial coaching fit call (to determine if we would be a good match), Violet shared that her main goal for coaching was to manage her bosses' perceptions and help them see that she deserved a more senior-level title. While she used the language of leadership change, she demonstrated little interest in soliciting feedback from others to help her understand her leadership growth areas.

Within the first sixty minutes of meeting Violet, there were already warning flags regarding her readiness for coaching:

- Her motivation was not to change herself but to change others.
- There was a sense of entitlement around a higher-level title and position (something she was owed), and she lacked the humility to learn why she'd not been given that role.
- Violet lacked curiosity about her growth areas and blind spots.

In the end, I suggested to Violet that this might not be the right time for coaching—at least with me—and perhaps it would be helpful if she revisited her coaching goals with her boss. I never heard from her again.

If we were to analogize these two leader examples to endurance athletics, we would hear one athlete reflecting something close to Michael Jordan's mentality: a burning desire to be at their best, to be pushed to fail so they can learn, and humility to know they are not above learning from others. The other is a high-performing person who can use all the language of their sport and put the uniform on, but on game day, wants the rules to be changed to their advantage. They believe they are already performing at the top of the game, and if that isn't reflected in the scoreboard, the scoreboard should be altered. If you are a professional sports fan, you can probably cite several examples of this kind of athlete.

Before you jump into the extensive interview of prospective coaches, take time to inspect your own motivations and readiness for coaching (see Figure 15).

Figure 15. Coaching Readiness Checklist

Ready for Coaching	Not Ready for Coaching
Motivated to improve or enhance my current leadership capabilities	Motivated to manage others' perceptions or to meet others' expectations for coaching
Self-aware enough to recognize I own the change I want to see	Externalizing responsibility for my current situation to others or the environment
Humble and strong enough to receive harsh feedback from my coach and colleagues	Too proud or fragile to take critical feedback, even if its sole intention is to make me better
Interested in learning about my strengths and weaknesses and how they contribute to my success	Overly focused on leveraging strengths; avoidance of or minimization of weaknesses
Tolerance for ambiguity and not knowing	Focused on tools and tricks rather than thinking broadly about self and leadership
The courage to do deep reflection, tapping into emotion and psychology to surface meaningful insights	More interested in seeking direction and advice than doing deep work
Willing to devote resources to the coaching effort (time, energy, mindshare, money)	Don't have the bandwidth/time/money to devote to coaching
Discipline to remain relentlessly committed to coaching goals despite obstacles and hardships	History of changing priorities quickly and moving on to the next new thing
Willing to be loud and proud about coaching with colleagues at all levels	Worried about what others will think when being coached

Having a coach can be one of the most valuable experiences an endurance leader will have. Make the most of it by critically evaluating your motives, the coaches you meet, and the realities of your current environment.

Coach's Questions ▬ ▬ ▬ ▬ ▬ ▬ ▬ ▬ ▬

- How could a coach help you achieve greater long-term leadership effectiveness?

- What Style of Coaching quadrant do you need?

- What coach qualities are a must-have versus nice-to-have for you?

- Is now the right time for you to leverage a coach? How could you know?

- What changes would you need to make to ensure you have enough time/energy/resources to devote to a coaching engagement?

- Are you ready for the challenging mental and psychological work of coaching?

Training Plan

- Determine if you are at a place in your leadership journey where using a coach would be particularly valuable. Are any of these true for you?

  - I want to improve my current leadership style to be more effective in my current role.
  - I want to prepare for a future role and build new leadership capabilities to get there.
  - I may have some development areas I don't understand well and need help to uncover.

- If any of the above are accurate, use the worksheet in Figure 15 to determine your readiness to engage in coaching. If most of your answers fall on the right side of the page, you have some internal work to do before you maximize the benefit of a coaching engagement.

- If you are ready for a coach, talk with your boss to ensure you have their endorsement and support (organizational, emotional, and financial). Then, use your peers, network, or human resources department to help you identify and source coaches. Ensure you know any specific processes or coach cadre the company wants you to use.

- Interview at least three coaches to determine which one is the best fit for you. Use Figure 14 to help you vet candidates.

- Make excellent use of coaching. Give it the respect and priority it deserves. If you do, you will make gains in your leadership that you may not have known possible.

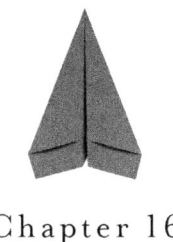

Chapter 16

Make Anyone A Coach

I am a success today because I had a friend who believed in me,
and I didn't have the heart to let him down.

ABRAHAM LINCOLN

Coaching Requires Multiple Perspectives

As discussed, formal coaches are an excellent resource for helping you improve your performance. However, the hours available in the coaching engagement limit their ability to observe you in your daily working environment. Unless your leadership coach is in-house, they will spend 20 percent or less of their time observing you in leadership interactions. This is a significant departure from athlete coaching, where coaches frequently observe their athletes in various situations and conditions.

Further, leadership coaching may not have access to the rich data available from the perspectives of those who work with the leader regularly. If the only coaching inputs are those provided by the leader and the only source of support is from the coach, this coaching team can unknowingly get lulled into a too-rosy notion of what is happening in the leader's ecosystem. To guard against following the primrose path of selectively constructed narratives about leader behavior, coaching should take advantage of the perspectives available within and outside the coach-leader dyad that can shed valuable light on how the leader is showing up.

Sometimes, those perspectives can come from unexpected places. For example, a few years ago, I was watching highlights from Ironman Austria. The race was grueling: pouring rain all day, creating miserable conditions. During the run portion of the race, one of the pro racers found himself walking—unthinkable for these elite athletes who must maintain a swift run pace to finish in the top tier. While he limped along miserably, a female everyday athlete ran by and said something to the elite racer. I don't know what she said, but it got him running. He picked up his pace, and then, in a flash, he was right behind her, then next to her. They ran together for a split second, and then he passed her. While he did not win the race, whatever she said gave him the boost to continue his mission and finish in a far better position than he would have otherwise.

Any athlete who is part of a team gives and receives feedback regularly because they know it will help them improve. Barton and Sutcliffe's 2023 study of adventure racers found, "Resilience was accomplished and re-accomplished through processes of interrelating, in which racers worked together to mutually adjust roles and engagement, coordinated through distributed sensemaking."[103] Without constant feedback, team members could misinterpret the information in their environment and make potentially disastrous (and, in some cases, deadly) mistakes.

Studies show that groups regularly outperform individuals in survival simulations, proof positive of the adage, "If you want to go fast, go alone; if you want to go far, go with others." Endurance leaders realize that to lead for decades successfully, they need a lot of input, feedback, and support. Otherwise, they may blaze brightly like a meteor and burn out just as quickly. Feedback from team members, bosses, peers, and even family members is critical for improvement and longevity.

Varied Feedback Makes You Invariably Better

Being willing to be coached is a necessary quality of elite performers and a core concept for endurance leaders. An essential part of being coached is receiving regular feedback, not only from the coach but also from others. Whether it is direct input from a peer or watching highlights of a competitor finish a race, feedback helps us understand where, how, and when we can improve. If athletes/leaders never get input from peers, they miss input from valuable sources that will ultimately make them better across different environments.

Unfortunately, most leaders tend to concern themselves solely with feedback from one source: their superiors. This may seem natural since direct bosses are the ones who often determine promotions and salary increases. However, bosses tend to prioritize the ability to get results over how the leader interacts with colleagues or manages direct reports. This is why some professionals are overpromoted; they have exceptional technical skills and get impressive results but lack the people skills to build great followership.

Exacerbating the problem is that this feedback is usually only collected once per year, at performance review time. That means a leader could go twelve months without receiving any feedback about their leadership performance. It would be like a Boston Marathon entrant training for an entire year without any feedback about their training. How would they know if they are doing the right things? How will they know if they are ready for the challenge of that arduous event?

Avoiding The Echo Chamber

While there's the old saying, "It is lonely at the top," there is also an echo chamber at the top. Executives and C-suite leaders can overlook the importance of getting feedback from various perspectives. Consciously or not, over time, they can surround themselves with people who do not challenge them enough and are unwilling to address bad behavior. This can contribute to what Stanford professor Bob Sutton calls "the fallacy of centrality," where leaders assume that because of their success, they know everything they need to know about the organization. This fallacy can lead to what Sutton calls "oblivious leadership."[104]

We can all think of examples of professional athletes and high-visibility CEOs who were unwilling to listen to the input of those around them. Ben Roethlisberger, a star quarterback in NFL football some years ago, is often mentioned as someone unable to learn from his peers or fans. Closing himself off from the better parts of public engagement, he seemed to isolate himself in a world where his only interactions with everyday people landed him in trouble. Legal woes plagued him and contributed to his demise on the field.[105] In the leadership space, Enron founder Ken Lay and CFO Jeff Skilling ignored employee warnings of financial mishandling at the energy giant. They surrounded themselves with people who only told them what they wanted to hear and walled themselves off from the information, leading to Enron's collapse (and their subsequent prison sentences). Intentionally oblivious leadership has its risks.

On the other hand, examples of intentionally cognizant leaders come from people like Harold MacDowell, CEO of TD Industries. While his name may not have immediate recognition, he has been at the helm of TD since 2005. He continues a tradition that began with the first two TD CEOs: hosting regular spaghetti dinners at his house with employees. MacDowell believes this is a great way to learn directly from his people about their experiences in the company.[106] As great CEOs know, seeking and acting on feedback from unexpected places can elevate organizational performance beyond what can be learned in the boardroom.

Feedback And Success (Or Lack Thereof)

As a consultant and coach, I have watched some top performers ignore feedback with harmful effects. For example, I coached a regional sales leader, Eduardo, early in my coaching career. Every day, Eduardo would enter his office building, breeze by his staff, and immediately go into his office and shut his door. This behavior was highlighted in his 360-degree evaluation (we discussed this as a baseline tool earlier) as an example of being out of touch with the people around him.

To change his behavior and others' experience of him, Eduardo began saying hello to his team members and asking them about their families and weekends. However, while his behavior had changed, his mindset did not. Eduardo did not indicate a genuine interest in the interactions; instead, according to his employees, he phoned them in. This did more harm than good to the trust people felt in him. Moreover, it cut him off from the valuable feedback the team around him possessed. Despite my efforts, I was unsuccessful in helping him change his mindset. Within a year after we worked together, Eduardo was removed from his role for underperformance.

Maureen, a manufacturing CEO we met earlier, is on the opposite end of the spectrum. Maureen believed that all employees added value. She spent the first part of her day, every day, walking around the plant and talking with employees. She would join the IT team's planning sessions. She would take groups of employees to lunch. She looked for feedback everywhere it could be found and would take that input to heart.

As a company in a competitive space, with needs for rapid technological advancement and fast prototyping, she leveraged what she learned from day-to-day employees to make intelligent, rapid changes to the business and her leadership. Six years after we met, Maureen and her team had grown the company tenfold and successfully sold it to the premier company in the industry.

Feedback Makes Anyone A Coach

To avoid one-dimensional feedback, I encourage leaders to use those around them as coaches. Here are a few tools that can help endurance leaders capture feedback from multiple points of view.

Multi-rater Feedback

As discussed earlier, this tool provides leaders with information on their behavior, helping them (and their coach) articulate work areas. It creates a solid, objective baseline of information, and participants can be re-engaged later to provide comparative data.

The other wonderful thing about multi-rater feedback is that it turns your participants into informal coaches. I've observed an interesting psychological phenomenon from working with multi-rater input over the years: when participants believe the leader is credible and motivated to improve their leadership, they become positively invested in the leader's change efforts. They want the leader to succeed. Great leaders take advantage of that support by using that feedback as a foot in the door to future feedback.

Allow me to illustrate. I introduced you to Peggy some time ago. When Peggy received her multi-rater feedback, she learned that her lack of a poker face created stress and sometimes intimidation in team meetings. Peggy brought that development area to key direct reports for more information and coaching.

She presented it to them each this way, "One of the things I learned from my feedback was that my physical reactions to frustrations or disappointments stress people out. Can you help me see this more clearly? When was the last meeting you observed me do that? What happened to you or others in that situation?" She asked for feedback through open-ended questions so her employees would not feel defensive. Had Peggy asked, "Have you seen this or not?" she would have created a situation where her direct reports would have to decide if it was safe to be honest with their boss. And it might have exacerbated any sense of intimidation they might have felt.

Peggy then took the feedback opportunity one step further: She asked a few team members if they would help her improve by signaling her when they saw her grimace or eye roll. One agreed to cough, and another to scratch the side of his nose. These team members became Peggy's real-time coaches in those meetings. She could course-correct on the spot by providing her with real-time feedback. Within two weeks, she was getting feedback from people that she seemed calmer and more positive in most team meetings.

Multi-rater feedback has great formal benefits but can also help leaders get more data from their stakeholders, providing more clarity, dialogue, and support.

Feedforward

Another technique to make anyone a coach is called "feedforward." Developed by world-renowned coach Marshall Goldsmith,[107] it is a straightforward and informal method of soliciting specific behavioral information from stakeholders. It offers a compelling alternative to feedback in that instead of using a backward-looking method, feedforward is a *future-oriented* process. It consists of two questions that a leader asks a colleague/boss/direct report:

- "What is one leadership behavior you've seen me exhibit well in the past month?"
- "What is one leadership behavior you would like to see me improve upon in the next month?"

The beauty of this approach is that it avoids asking awkward questions about past behavior, freeing the colleague up to speak openly and positively about what to do next. Another benefit of feedforward is that it can be used frequently without creating survey fatigue by stakeholders. Being asked these same two questions once per month is a five-minute investment with countless upsides for the leader.

Group Feedforward

One excellent group or team activity is group feedforward. In this exercise, I give each group member a piece of paper (see Figure 16). At the top of the page, I have them write down one thing they want to improve in their leadership. Then, I divide the group into pairs. Person A shares their goal with Person B, and Person B gives them one idea for how to improve it. Person A writes that idea on their sheet, saying thank you and nothing else. Then they switch: Person B tells Person A what they want to improve, and Person A gives them one idea. Person B writes that down. Then, they pair up with a completely different person in the room, and the process starts again.

My favorite way to do this activity is in lightning rounds; in other words, no more than two minutes per pairing. It forces people to be quick in their questions and subsequent responses. By the time the rounds are done, each leader has several ideas for improving in this area. People love this activity because it provides unfettered access to various perspectives they might otherwise miss. Even when the other person doesn't know the leader well, it never fails that they can still provide them with something useful. I encourage you to try it with your team and see what responses you get.

Figure 16. Feedforward Worksheet

Behavior To Change	
	Feedforward
Name 1	
Name 2	
Name 3	
Name 4	
Name 5	
Name 6	
Name 7	
Name 8	
Name 9	

Feedback Through Mentoring

Another strategy for making anyone a coach is through mentoring. While coaching and mentoring are different tools, they both provide the irreplaceable benefit of perspective from others. Allow me to share a powerful mentorship example of my own. Some time ago, I received hours of counsel from two perspectives regarding proposing work to a potential client. The priceless advice was not from a paid consultant but from peer mentors. They each provided valuable insight regarding approaching the work proposal. Just a few hours before the calls, I'd felt adrift and anxious about how to respond to the opportunity; after the calls, I felt energized and equipped with a thoughtful, well-informed game plan.

Over the past few years, I've become increasingly invested in seeking mentorship. I have a few theories as to why. One theory is that because I am a sole proprietor and a strong extrovert in a work-from-home world, I often long for camaraderie in what can sometimes be a lonely existence. I have brilliant colleagues and contemporaries—why not tap into that source of insight regularly? Another theory is that because I am the youngest of seven children, I have always benefitted from excellent mentorship within my immediate family. Whatever the reason, I have little interest in going it alone these days. I prefer to turn to peers and senior members of my profession to build superior consulting skills and personal relationships to ensure I live my life aligned with my ultimate mission.

Overcoming The Obstacles To Mentorship

The wonderful thing about mentoring is it is a win-win. For both parties, it enhances our thinking, creates clarity and perspective, expands our network, and provides us with more visibility—all of which could lead to better leadership, enhanced career opportunities, or more fulfilling life goals. Sounds like a win-win, right? So, why does finding a mentor seem so difficult? Nod if any of the following describe you:

- Your work environment does not provide exposure or time to leverage potential mentors.
- Mentoring has become an overly complex or formal process within your work environment (e.g., matching systems, structured meeting requirements, and reporting out) that it doesn't seem worth it.
- Working from home makes it hard to find and connect with potential mentors.
- The ratio of mentees to mentors is about 162:1 (or that's what it feels like). Finding a mentor who will provide you with time can be challenging.
- You'd love to have a mentor but are too busy (or you think your potential mentor is too busy).
- You don't know where to start, who to ask, or what to do.

If you feel stuck in this mentoring riptide, take heart. There are likely excellent mentors around you—with no formal process, fees, or programs required. To help you find your way, determine a few things:

- *What do you want out of mentorship?* Are you looking for a guide for life, or perhaps just for next year? Do you need someone for a particular point in time to help you through a challenging situation like a job transition, a new leadership role, or managing a challenging conflict? Do you want a mentor who will meet regularly or with whom you can have impromptu/point-in-time discussions?
- *Who qualifies as a mentor?* Must you have the CEO as a mentor to feel like it is a valuable use of your time? Probably not. Perhaps it is a colleague, a seasoned veteran of your business, or the twenty-something whiz-kid leading your department in innovation. One litmus test to determine if someone is a good mentor is asking yourself, "Can I learn some essential things from this person?" If so, consider using them.

- *What do you offer?* Is there a case to be made for why this person would spend their most precious commodity (their free time) with you? What will they get out of the deal? The less the person knows you, the more you may have to make that an explicit part of the ask. If you can't find anything of value to give to the mentor, it may be the wrong person to approach. On the other hand, you may need to build your confidence and recognize what you bring to the relationship.

Once you've determined your internal parameters for mentorship, do the following:

- *Determine the optimal structure of the relationship.* The graph (see Figure 17)[108] shows diverse types of mentorships. You might focus on just one domain or want to engage each one. The right composition will depend on the time and energy investment you and any mentor are willing to make.

- Figure 17. Types Of Mentoring

- *Look around you.* Examine who in your life is already providing you with mentorship. Chances are, there is someone you are already leveraging for their knowledge, expertise, honesty, listening skills, and willingness to challenge you. Determine how you want to leverage their expert capabilities and make this an explicit part of the relationship—and what you will offer them in exchange.

- *Know the limits.* Sometimes, the counsel and support you can get from a mentoring relationship isn't enough; you might need more robust training or consultation (e.g., advanced education, certifications, therapy, or formal supervision). Have a candid conversation with your mentor if your needs aren't getting met; the chances are good that they feel similar. They may even have resources to help you achieve your next goal.

- *Be a mentor.* One of the best ways to expand your expertise is to mentor others. Being challenged, questioned, and asked for your expertise will bolster your knowledge and confidence. Iron sharpens iron. It's also a great way to pay it forward for all the tremendous mentoring you will receive over your lifetime.

The Grace To Receive

Asking for feedback is hard; receiving difficult feedback you weren't expecting is even more challenging. Endurance leaders embrace both, knowing both conditions will help them with their long-term success. As Marshall Goldsmith says, "Feedback is a gift." Think of it like any other gift: when given to you, you graciously accept it and say, "Thank you."[109] It means having the humility to recognize there is always room to improve things and graciously receiving input to achieve higher performance.

Good feedback receivers don't explain, defend, or blame; they are grateful to the feedback giver and take accountability for making changes (which is the ultimate show of gratitude). It means being willing to shed preconceived notions about the status of the giver, such as being too junior or not as intelligent, experienced, or savvy as you. Recognizing that every person you encounter probably has something worthwhile to share is a critical perspective to keep you improving long after you've made it.

Endurance leaders recognize that getting closer to their short- and long-term goals and living their ultimate mission requires coaching from various sources. They seek those out, get curious and humble, and leverage those inputs to their full advantage. If someone runs up beside you when you're struggling and whispers some encouragement, will you have the courage to listen and respond?

Coach's Questions ▬ ▬ ▬ ▬ ▬ ▬ ▬ ▬ ▬ ▬ ▬

- Looking back over your career, what are some of the most valuable pieces of feedback you've received? From whom did you receive them? How did they change you?

- Who do you currently use as a coach? When and how do you use them? Could you be using more or better sources of coaching?

- What coaching/mentoring strategies make the most sense for you right now? How can you build that into your regular professional development?

- How do you tend to respond when someone gives you spontaneous feedback? What could make you better at receiving it?

- Where are you looking for your next leadership lesson?

- Whose voice are you not seeking? How could you change that?

Training Plan

- List how you've received feedback and coaching in the past three years. Are they all through formal means, e.g., performance reviews or multi-rater feedback? If so, make an intentional plan to seek out informal feedback and pick a strategy for getting it.

- Think of three people whose perspective would benefit you, but you are not seeking. Ask them for some feedforward or feedback. And don't forget to say thank you.

- Try the feedforward questions or group feedforward sheet (see Figure 16) to help you improve on a focus area.

- List out your current mentors. Who would you like to have on this list? Plan to advocate for yourself to obtain that perspective.

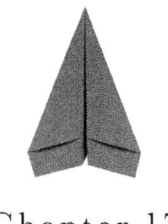

Chapter 17

Fall In Love With Metrics

*Don't measure anything unless the data helps you make
a better decision or change your actions.*
SETH GODIN

Tracking Our Lives

It's almost overwhelming when you think about all the ways technology
has become embedded in our lives. Some have been around for a while
and feel as natural as breathing, like your phone, internet browsers, and
social media accounts. Some are designed to make our home and work
lives more manageable, while others help with physical wellness. Some are
less obvious, like scanning your items at the self-checkout in the grocery
store, pulling into the parking garage, or entering a concert arena. And all
these technologies we love? They are tracking us. We may pretend not to
notice because the idea of being followed at every turn is disconcerting.
But make no mistake—the partners we invite into our lives via technology
have access to much about our lives. They use our information to create
big data such as consumer spending habits, household trends, and global
energy usage. Big data helps companies, communities, and governments
make organizational and business decisions.

We also track much in our work worlds. SMART goals (specific, measurable, achievable, relevant, and time-bound), KPIs (key performance indicators), project plans, monthly or weekly team and individual performance evaluations, quarterly business reports, and company earnings reports are just a few of the tracking tools that organizations use to ensure they are moving toward their short- and long-term plans. We accept these tracking tools without question.

Are we as comfortable or well-versed in tracking the critical metrics for our ultimate mission? In 2010, the late researcher, innovator, endurance leader, and devout Mormon, Clayton M. Christiansen, wrote a famous *Harvard Business Review* article, "How will you measure your life?" In it, he highlights the fundamental lack of purpose he sees Harvard Business School students have when they arrive on campus. He challenges them to think about what is truly most important in their lives for the long term: their happiness, families, and integrity.[110] He challenges them to articulate something akin to the ultimate mission. He argues that without those clear definitions, we can get lured into yardsticks of success that may be important to others or the world but are meaningless to us.

Why Mission Is Hard To Track

Our technological capabilities make it easy to acclimate to numerically focused work objectives. Yet, we do not always take the time to pursue long-term success metrics that are tied to our purpose. Why is that?

- *It's unfamiliar.* Determining if we are on the road to achieving our ultimate mission can be more complicated than deciding if the team is meeting the month's sales quota. We will likely meet our quota if we follow clearly defined activities such as meeting with potential and current customers, using established sales practices, and managing our sales pipeline effectively. The link to success in our long-term goals may be more indirect. For example, we may aim to make a meaningful and distinct contribution to society, but we find we're not getting as much time to contribute to community service as we'd like. Did we define our path to success too narrowly? Is there another way to meet that societal contribution goal, such as spending more time in coaching efforts with the team you lead? Getting it right can take time because there aren't hard and fast rules for defining success.

- *It can be challenging to get accurate feedback.* Work goals have clear timelines for delivery, and we are likely to get immediate feedback if we meet or fail to meet them. We can solicit feedback from our boss or others who clearly know what success should look like. However, it can be difficult for others to evaluate where we are on our mission-focused goals. Can your colleague observe if you are managing your schedule effectively and making necessary time for reflection? Probably not. So, we tend to go it alone and assume we can get there on our own. You know how that goes.

- *The metrics are "squishy."* Trying to focus on long-term leadership success and your ultimate mission has a lot to do with life satisfaction and goals that may be hard to see but easy to feel. Not only is this difficult for some people to grasp, but generations of leaders have been taught that squishy/emotional things are weak, especially in the workplace. That sentiment can be hard to break.

While all these reasons have merit, they may prevent you from finding value in using reasonably-sourced metrics to help you determine if you are becoming more of the endurance leader you desire.

Metrics To Achieve Long-Term Goals

Show me a committed endurance athlete, and I'll show you someone obsessed with metrics. I confess to being a bit of a data junkie myself. I've been spotted at formal gala events sporting my big, clunky Garmin triathlon watch with the aquamarine-colored sports band. I look at my phone for my Training Peaks updates after every workout. But my obsession has helped me become a better athlete, and I'm not alone.

Sika Henry is a corporate analyst and the first Black professional triathlete; she is also on the list of the top US-born Black female marathoners.[111] In 2020, Henry reached her goal of finishing a marathon in under three hours (well under seven minutes per mile). But she had come a long way from her first-ever marathon finish of 3 hours 58 minutes in 2007. Henry dedicated considerable time and attention to improving her running, and a big part of that was paying attention to data. In describing her record-breaking marathon finish, she states that her coach had her focused on a negative split, which means running the second half of a race faster than the first. This was difficult for Henry, as the top four women in the marathon started the race extremely fast, pacing under seven minutes per mile. But she had the discipline and focus to attend to the metrics and her plan rather than what her body might get tricked into doing due to the performance of those around her (remember our discussion of pacing?). Her coach had her racing for time, not placing on the podium. So, Henry carefully tracked her metrics at each mile, following the coach's advice, and did exactly what she was instructed.[112]

What Henry's story elucidates is that metrics can help you:

- Improve over time
- Focus on what is essential and not get distracted by irrelevant factors or competitions
- Get immediate feedback about your performance to your goal
- Stay true to a longer-term goal

A Wearable Coach

The use of wearable technology in the workplace is expanding at a rapid pace. In many cases, the goal is increased health and safety. For example, in 2020, during the height of the COVID-19 pandemic, Ford Motor Company piloted buzzing wristbands for workers to wear when they came within six feet of one another.[113] Other uses include helping workers make smart ergonomic decisions and keeping workers connected. Besides providing value for organizations, they also provide helpful information to leaders. Ruderman and Clerkin's research (2021) suggests that wearable technologies "can create ongoing opportunities for learning intrapersonal qualities relevant to leadership. In particular, they offer insights about using self-tracking to manage responses to stress and fatigue and for the delivery of verbal presentations."[114]

As an endurance leader interested in tracking metrics, you may find smartwatch technology an invaluable tool to approximate a personal coach. James L. McQuivey, a researcher at Forrester Research, called smartwatches "someone who knows more about what you need than you do."[115] That sounds an awful lot like the role of a coach. Coaches provide an invaluable resource in understanding our progress toward outstanding results. But the thing on our wrist may help us advance those goals by tracking our real-time progress.

Let's look at an example of health metrics tracking with an endurance leader. I had the opportunity to coach Astrid some time ago. Astrid was a president for a large European manufacturing company. Considered a high-potential candidate for global leadership, she had transformed some smaller-country commercial operations with immense success.

To continue to grow and expand her skills, Astrid had been moved to ever-larger countries to manage more complex business environments, and she was thriving. However, as her responsibilities grew, she found less and less time to prioritize health and well-being, particularly exercise and sleep. As a result, she felt that she wasn't as sharp cognitively and was having more difficulty managing daily stressors.

Along with some specific business focus areas, our coaching emphasized prioritizing these health areas. I tasked Astrid with tracking her sleep and exercise regimen each week. (She already had that data on her smartwatch, so extracting that information took no extra effort.) Her job was to take a screenshot of the week's sleep and exercise data on her phone and send it to me via text, along with her commentary on how it went. At first, she was shocked and a bit discouraged about what the data revealed. She said, "As soon as I paid attention and could see these numbers in black and white, I knew something had to change."

After just a few weeks of reporting her data to me, Astrid had already improved sleep and exercise: She slept closer to seven hours per night instead of six and found at least thirty minutes to exercise three to four times per week. She reported feeling years younger, with more energy, enthusiasm, and a calmer presence with her staff and others. She also said she found herself more present and available for her family because she felt less guilty and distracted. Tracking these simple metrics helped Astrid regain critical skills and reestablish priorities she'd lost sight of. They helped her regain the motivation and discipline to prioritize her health, a key element in her ability to meet her endurance leadership goals.

Let's look at an example from beyond health statistics and into direct leader behavior. A few years ago, I worked with an executive, Mae. Mae was a brilliant leader who had taken over a struggling organization and turned it around through directive leadership, disciplined processes, and rigorous accountability systems. She was well respected, but one of her worst qualities was her tendency to get frustrated and lose her temper in meetings with her team. Initially, she would become quiet, a behavior her team named "the calm before the storm."

After a few minutes, she would raise her voice, curse, or direct anger to an individual or the whole group. As a result, many people feared her and didn't fully trust her. Through some important multi-rater feedback, Mae recognized that this was getting in the way of her full leadership potential and wanted to change her behavior. She already used a smartwatch to track her steps, tell her when to get up and move, and receive email notifications. Leveraging the watch, we identified some critical biometric phenomena happening in those meetings: as her frustration rose, her heart rate would increase, and she would begin to sweat. (Does this sound like anything you may experience when frustrated or angry?)

Using the watch, we set some goals before her executive team meetings, which are high-stakes situations in which she often lost control.

- *Keep heart rate under control.* Mae's resting heart rate (HR) was seventy. We had her keep her Apple watch on the heart rate setting during the meetings. If she started feeling slightly annoyed, she glanced at her watch and noted her heart rate. If it was higher than eighty, she needed to do two to three relaxation breaths to bring it back to her resting heart rate before she could speak or ask a question. This gave her some control over what was going on and a short mental time out during the meeting so she could refocus her thinking in a positive direction.
- *Manage interaction.* Once she finished her relaxation breaths, Mae would start her stopwatch. She had three minutes to interject positively in the conversation by asking a clarifying question, affirming another leader's input, etc. After that, she needed to go no longer than ten percent of the meeting time (in a sixty-minute meeting, six minutes) without saying anything. This helped her find her voice rather than allowing her frustration to build.

Through these interventions, Mae began to find a new rhythm to her interactions with her team, much to their relief and group success. Eight years later, her team still tells me that her watch changed her whole meeting countenance.

In addition to examples like Mae's, I've encouraged leaders to use their phones or watches for tracking various metrics, among them:

- Productivity
- Time management
- Sleep hours and quality
- Stress levels throughout the day

- Screen time/social media time
- Alcohol intake
- Downtime

Artificial intelligence (AI) is being embedded in technologies to help leaders and teams track progress toward goals in areas such as:

- Communication style, tone, and frequency; listening vs. talking
- Executive presence
- Team engagement
- Delegation, feedback, motivation, and recognition of employees
- Conflict management and resolution
- Productivity and time management

To illustrate, in their 2024 *Harvard Business Review* article on the ways AI is changing team dynamics, Retiz and Higgins discuss a new technology called ReadAI: "Read AI (a smart AI tool that records, transcribes, and analyses interactions and incorporates into summaries) goes further [than tools on Teams and Zoom], measuring meeting participants' engagement, sentiment, and airtime. These applications can be integrated into work so seamlessly users begin to use them almost without realizing."[116] The technological innovation in metrics tracking is exploding, allowing you to track specific metrics around your leadership style and impact.

The Beauty Of Analog

While technology can be a fantastic tool, sometimes, one of the best strategies for tracking metrics is to go old-school; in other words, determining "How do you feel?" Endurance athletes know this as the rate of perceived exertion, or RPE. An athlete is asked to gauge their perceived effort level during a particular exercise or workout on a scale of one to ten. In other words, how hard was that workout, where one means incredibly easy and ten means all-out.

There is no set scale definition, so the athlete is left to determine on their own what constitutes easy or hard. But since it is used for a single athlete to measure their performance, there's internal consistency, which is what matters. RPE can do things no technology can: it allows athletes to examine how they feel, which might indicate something significant. For example, a marathon runner may complete a track workout with an RPE of four. The following week, the runner completes the same workout under similar conditions, but the RPE is eight. However, the watch metrics don't look that different week to week. The critical data is in the RPE: what caused the athlete to feel so differently from one week to the next? Is he more fatigued from recent workouts or a lack of sleep? Is his nutrition different? Does he have more work or personal stress? Is he sick or injured?

The answers to these questions will dramatically change how the athlete thinks about his following workouts. As one marathon blogger states, "No matter how good your [smart] device is, it can't tell you how you're feeling—what your level of motivation, or willpower, or fatigue is, on any given day. RPE does. It also stops you from being too prescriptive in the pace you're running; some days will be better or worse than others, and constantly trying to hit the same time or speed is often counterproductive."[117] I use RPE in coaching regularly and suggest that my endurance leaders also use it with their team members. It sounds like this: "Sam, you were working last week on spending more time managing and empowering your team than worrying about completing tasks yourself. On a scale of one to ten, with one being terrible and ten being as good as you could have done, how did it go?" We have just created an RPE-like metric. We did not capture Sam's exact minutes in team leadership activities, but we got a sense of where he thinks he is. We can now talk about how we might move that number (whatever it is) up one notch next week and repeat the process when we next speak.

Leaders do not need a coach to track RPE; it can easily be part of a regular action-reflection cycle or a daily review. The important thing is to regularly check in on behavior changes and annotate how you are doing. This can help nip problems in the bud if your numbers are declining or seek help or coaching if your numbers are stagnating. Remember, the more specific and granular the data, the easier it is to gauge if the metric is helping us move toward the desired change.

Appendix 1 shows the first page of the action planning form I send each leader as we begin working together. It encourages the leader to think about what success in coaching will look like, establish specific metrics that are meaningful to them, and start tracking their success.

Make Falling In Love Easy

Whether digital, smart, or analog, metrics tracking can help you see improvements as you build your endurance leadership. Metrics can also be incredibly motivating—nothing encourages continued improvement like past improvement. But they all come with risks, particularly smart technologies where privacy and security risks loom. They also can lose meaning if individuals find themselves so wrapped up in the data that they lose sight of the goal. If you are considering a new strategy to track progress toward your endurance leader goals, research the best and safest tools to fit your needs.

The bottom line is to find meaningful tracking strategies (i.e., those that tie in with your ultimate mission) that work with your personality and lifestyle. To remain consistent, pick solutions you can use with little friction. Doing so will make falling in love with metrics tracking much easier. So, what are you waiting for? Find something easy to track and start there; your future leadership self will thank you.

Coach Questions

- Thinking about your ultimate mission and training plan, what are a few discrete and reasonable behaviors you want to target to achieve your goals?

- How and when will those behaviors be measured?

- What internal or external strategies can you use to help track progress easily and meaningfully?

- Who can help you stay accountable to your chosen metrics and ensure they help you progress toward your goals?

- How can you stay true to what's meaningful to you (i.e., how will you measure your life)?

Training Plan

- Select two specific plans you've developed to improve in a critical leadership area. Determine one metric for gauging your success in each plan. If you use SMART goals, you may have already articulated that; if not, figure out what success might look like.

- Decide how, when, and where you will track your metrics. Will you use smart technology, RPE, or feedback from others? When will you give yourself the time and space to review these metrics and sufficiently plan your next steps?

- Articulate your metrics to someone and tell them your plan for tracking them. This may increase your sense of accountability.

- Try out Appendix 1. Share the results with your boss, coach, or other person helping you stay accountable. Make sure to keep this a working document you check in on regularly to keep it meaningful.

Chapter 18

Cultivating Gratitude

No one who achieves success does so without the help of others.
The wise and confident acknowledge this help with gratitude.
ALFRED NORTH WHITEHEAD

Joy In The Journey

One of my longtime Ironman heroes is former world champion and legend Chrissy Wellington. Wellington was known for her incredible speed and competitive, won't-lose attitude. Combined with a hefty dose of humility, an approachable disposition, and a million-watt smile, she emanated warmth while crushing races.

I had the privilege to see Wellington race up close when volunteering at Ironman Arizona years ago. She came out of the water after a lightning-fast swim time and was well ahead of her competitors as she ran to the first transition area to get on her bike. As she sprinted by the volunteers on her way, she broke out her signature grin and, waving vigorously, yelled, "Hi, guys!" We all whooped and cheered not only at her considerable lead but also at the fact that she took the time to acknowledge us in such an effusive manner. Many racers would be so focused on their next move that they would barely glance at the volunteers they passed. At worst, I've seen pro athletes scream at volunteers or other racers who are not doing what they might want. Wellington's attitude inspired not only those around her, but they also seemed to inspire her. Early in her racing career, she realized that smiling and cheering on the spectators and her fellow competitors helped her to race better.

Whenever Wellington raced, she was having fun and doing what she loved. Yes, it was work, but there was nowhere else she wanted to be, perhaps because she had stumbled upon the sport more than twenty years ago while working as a civil servant in her native Australia.

One author describing Wellington says, "The smile was genuine. The joy was heartfelt. 'I was so grateful to have found something I was good at—a talent I didn't know I had,' [Wellington] says. 'I was so excited!'"[118] In her book, *A Life Without Limits*, Wellington cites the ongoing inspiration of her father's parting advice when dropping her off to begin university: "Just seize every opportunity you have, embrace every experience. Make a mark for all the right reasons."[119] Her reflections on success are filled with gratitude and credits her success to that gratitude.

Gratitude And Success

Why would we list gratitude as part of leveraging support? It is your self-support system, an internal flotation device you can activate to keep you buoyed on your long-term leadership journey. It is a critical component of true success. Sir Richard Branson often speaks of happiness as the key to his business and financial success, not vice versa. He talks regularly about the importance of maintaining gratitude for the life we've been given and being of service to others—not gratitude only in the reflective moments, but gratitude when life becomes challenging.

John C. Maxwell says, "Gratitude is one of the most important components of leadership, and it's essential for lifetime growth. Remember this: What we appreciate appreciates, and what we depreciate depreciates."[120] In other words, the things in life we take the time to acknowledge and be grateful for tend to grow in value—not only for ourselves but for those around us. And the things that we don't appreciate lose their value. This is tricky for most of us because it implies that when we don't pay attention to things or people around us, they will be devalued. There is no middle ground here; we are building up or allowing things to erode. Ignoring will ultimately devalue people or things. If you own anything of material value, you can understand this. It will eventually break down if you do not put time and effort into maintaining that item.

Bouchirka's 2024 article highlights thirty-five research articles showing the profound benefits of gratitude: physical health benefits like improved sleep and motivation to exercise; mental, psychological, and spiritual health benefits such as improved self-confidence, decreased envy and jealousy, and enhanced resilience; and workplace benefits, such as increased productivity and better decision-making skills.[121] In other words, the benefits of gratitude extend beyond personal health, well-being, and physical performance. Research also shows that gratitude can improve your leadership qualities (confidence, decision-making) and impact (productivity). Endurance leaders will do well to pursue cultivating gratitude to enhance their personal and professional performance.

The Physical Impact Of Stress

Unfortunately, many leaders struggle to engage in an attitude of gratitude regularly. With the relentless pressures of today's business environment, they are not often able to seize a moment but may instead feel seized by it. They can feel depleted of joy rather than having an opportunity to revel in it. Even when leaders feel good for a fleeting moment, the next deadline suddenly looms, goals are changed, or a problematic team member throws them back into a world of crisis management. Sights get lowered, expectations shortened, stress increases, and survival instincts rise. Stress interferes with success.

When we perceive an immediate threat, our body engages in what is known as our acute stress response. This activates several internal systems to keep us alive: our sympathetic nervous system engages epinephrine and norepinephrine, and our adrenal system produces up to thirty excess endorphins and hormones like oxytocin and testosterone. These flood our bloodstream to prepare us for one of four responses: fight, flight, freeze, or fawn (fawn is an attempt to please someone to reduce threat). Once the danger is diminished, our parasympathetic nervous system kicks in to bring us back to normalcy by releasing endorphins, dopamine, and serotonin. But it takes much longer to get back to normal than it did to get stressed in the first place. If we remain in a continued state of stress (or chronic stress as it is known), it gets harder and harder to return to baseline, which can lead to a host of adverse mental and physical health problems.

As leaders, remaining in an elevated state of stress inhibits our ability to focus on anything other than the short term. Remember, these are ancient survival instincts—they are just trying to keep you alive at the moment—they don't care about next year. As a result, our long-term efforts can get thwarted, and our focus on outstanding leadership and team collaboration can be put on the back burner. We remain in a continuous loop of short-term, often counterproductive behavior.

Stress, Interrupted

One of the best ways to interrupt this cycle is to engage the parasympathetic system more quickly by sending the body and the brain messages that they are safe. Danger and gratitude are mutually competing mental processes: gratitude requires acknowledging something other than this moment and experiencing a feeling of abundance. Neurochemistry supports acts of giving: Research shows that when we give, our adrenal glands activate parasympathetic hormones to help us return to normalcy. On the other hand, danger activates a scarcity mentality and the inability to focus on anything other than this moment. Practicing gratitude makes you more likely to ward against mild and chronic stress risks.

Gratitude has been well studied as a mediating variable in sports performance. Gabana et al. (2017) found a negative correlation between gratitude and burnout and a positive correlation between gratitude and athletes' satisfaction with their sport.[122] In another 2017 study, researchers found that across cultures, athletes with higher levels of gratitude showed more life satisfaction when they had increased levels of mindfulness.[123] By being mindful of what they are grateful for, the athletes seemed to feel better about life.

I had a personal experience of this a few years ago. I was competing in a half-Ironman race in North Carolina on a sweltering day in early October. I'd completed the swim and bike portions of the race, and I was now on the 13.1-mile run portion. I'm not a great runner, and I tend to get very negative in my head when the weather is too hot. I was trying to execute many endurance leader lessons, like running the mile I was in, managing my pace, etc. But I was still struggling to escape woe is me.

Around mile six, I saw a friend coming the other way, who whooped and cheered for me. Shortly after that, I saw my husband volunteering at the water aid station, and he did the same. After those two buoying moments, I knew I was facing six long miles without much external positivity. I realized that to keep my spirits up, I needed to share that cheering I'd just experienced.

So, I began aggressively cheering for my fellow racers along the other way. I started clapping and whooping, especially when I saw someone who looked hot and miserable (basically everyone). What I got in return was a ton of smiles, several "thank you!" or "you too!" messages, and sometimes a return of clapping and cheering. The result was a flood of gratitude in my heart and head: instead of focusing on the heat and the road ahead, I was saying to myself, "How incredible that you get to do this" and "Look at all these people out here giving their time away to allow us to be out here." I began focusing on how many people I could make smile. Somewhere, I was channeling Chrissie Wellington because I crossed that finish line with a big smile and a little leap in my step. Without practicing that gratitude, I doubt I would have finished as strongly as I did.

Gratitude In Leadership

Do you remember David? Despite his difficult start in life, David has become one of the most celebrated criminal defense attorneys in his state, written a compelling autobiography, and launched a successful recidivism reduction nonprofit. David has wealth, power, influence, and a beautiful family. Having built so much of that by pulling himself up by the bootstraps, it would be easy to expect David to be arrogant or at least have a large ego.

Yet, interacting with him, you would know nothing of his accomplishments. Whenever I speak with David, some of his first words are, "I'm so blessed and so grateful." A man of strong faith, he credits God for creating this rich life. He is also quick to heap praise on all those around him: his mentors, coach, and team members. Whenever I hear someone give David accolades, he immediately credits others. David does not merely practice gratitude; he embodies it.

Recently, David went through some personal difficulties. It would have been easy—and justifiable—for him to become angry, disillusioned, or distrustful of others. Other people in his situation might have become withdrawn or self-absorbed in their pain. While he did experience many of those feelings, David understood them to be temporary. Throughout it all, he maintained his focus on all the incredible blessings he had in life and leaned into those to help him through this rough patch. He has turned the setback into a learning opportunity and has grown closer to those involved rather than further away.

This hearkens back to Richard Branson's notion that stuff doesn't make you grateful or happy but vice versa. And true to John C. Maxwell's form, David's appreciation has helped me and others grow in appreciation for him.

In your journey to long-term success as a leader, you will encounter more than a few challenges, stresses, and losses. The more practiced you are in gratitude, the better prepared you will be to face them with a spirit of positivity and, perhaps, like Chrissie Wellington, a smile.

Cultivating Gratitude

Here are a few ways to start working on building gratitude. This is not an exhaustive list, but if you've not tried these strategies before, you may find them compelling. Like all new strategies, doing something that takes little time and fits into what you already do is critical to sticking with it. Use James Clear's method and try a 1 percent shift in gratitude; you'll be surprised where it takes you.

Gratitude Practice

- *Thank others habitually and specifically.* When we express gratitude directly to others, we acknowledge some humility (we couldn't do it all ourselves) and express appreciation for another. Win-win.
  - While saying, "Thanks for your help," is nice, it is even better for both parties to be specific. Try something like, "I appreciate your willingness to take time last week to help me think through that customer issue. Your ideas helped me think about the problem much differently, and I can now see a new way forward." Conveying that kind of impact makes the appreciation stickier for both of you.
  - Another technique for thanking others is to use the classic practice of a thank-you note. Decades ago, the CEO of the consulting firm I worked for, Frank Merritt, used to write six thank-you notes a week, as taught to him by his mentor. When asked why he did it, Frank would say it was more for him than for the recipient. While you may not be drawn to sitting down with pen and paper, sending an e-thank-you note or text message also works (although they do not provide the thrill of finding a fun handwritten gift in the mailbox).
- *Start a gratitude list or journal.* Simply annotating three things you are grateful for daily has been shown to boost immune function, help you sleep better, and create several additional health benefits. In a 2016 study of patients with Stage B heart failure (HF), Redwine

et al. concluded, "Gratitude journaling may improve biomarkers related to HF morbidity, such as reduced inflammation."[124] If gratitude journaling can reduce the risk of heart failure in specific populations, what could it do for you? There are thousands of ways to do this: it might be as small as a daily scrap piece of paper, as fancy as a beautifully bound journal, as old-school as pen and paper, or as tech-friendly as a gratitude app. Find a format that works for you, a time of day that makes sense (for most people, it's first thing in the morning), and build a small habit.

- *Start meetings and conversations with gratitude.* I've participated in several US Thanksgiving celebrations that have started with everyone going around the room and saying what they are grateful for. Often, this is a powerful—and sometimes emotional—moment. Could you imagine doing such a thing in a meeting? Well…maybe you should, as gratitude can help people feel fulfilled at work. The American Psychological Association's 2023 Work in America survey found that when people feel valued at work, they are more likely to make positive contributions, and the risk of quiet quitting decreases.[125]
  - Here are a few strategies:
    - Rather than start your weekly team meeting with check-ins, begin with everyone saying one thing they are grateful for.
    - Dedicate a wall or dry-erase board as a "shout-out" corner where people express gratitude for teammates' efforts, big and small. Ensure you (and other leaders) read and contribute to it frequently.
    - Find ways to add special recognition for extraordinary efforts: spot bonuses, small gifts, an extra day off, or even a catered lunch from a favorite deli can make individuals and teams feel recognized and important.
- *Volunteer.* There is nothing like giving your time and talent to others to make you acutely aware of how good you have it. Like

other gratitude practices, volunteering has been found to have physical and mental health benefits, such as lowering blood pressure, reducing anxiety and depression, and living longer. Additionally, a 2021 study found that volunteering increased subjects' reports of subjective well-being. This is important because it shows that it isn't that happier people volunteer, but volunteering makes people happier.[126] In a recent Mayo Clinic article, clinical social worker Angela Thoreson states, "Volunteering reduces stress and increases positive, relaxed feelings by releasing dopamine. By spending time in service to others, volunteers report feeling a sense of meaning and appreciation, both given and received, which can have a stress-reducing effect."[127]

- While financial contributions can be an excellent way to express gratitude, some recent research found that volunteering has a slightly stronger association with psychological well-being than charitable donations.[128] Giving oneself directly seems to help people feel good in ways that cannot be replicated through financial support.

- Finding the time, energy, and direction to volunteer can be challenging. Some suggested ways to get started:
  - Find an organization that has personal meaning to you and look at their volunteer opportunities.
  - Use skills you already have. Do you have an MBA in finance? Perhaps dedicate time to helping teach financial literacy to at-risk young adults or keep the financial records for your local historical association (as my ninety-year-old mother does).
  - Make it a "win-win" event—schedule a service day for your family or team to allow others to volunteer and build relationships.

Remember what John C. Maxwell said about appreciation appreciating. Spending time in gratitude can help us live more intently on the bright side, keep us physically and mentally strong, and reduce and manage stress. It is a secret weapon you have on your endurance journey—use it liberally and share it with others. It will make you even stronger.

Coach Questions

- What benefits can you see to cultivating gratitude as a person and a leader?

- What are some ways you like to express gratitude now? When and how do you do it?

- How could a more consistent gratitude practice help future-proof your leadership?

- Where is one place you would like to express gratitude more regularly (e.g., with family, friends, at work)? What would the impact of that gratitude be on those around you?

Training Plan

- At this very moment, stop reading and write down three things you are grateful for. Now, read those and reflect for a moment. What happened to your heart rate? Your blood pressure? Your facial expression? How long did that activity take? Can you find a way to embed that into a daily practice?

- Make a stress-interruption plan using gratitude: develop a strategy for invoking gratitude when your stress level increases (e.g., increased heart rate, racing thoughts). It may be writing or articulating something you are grateful for out loud. Try it and see if your recovery time from that stress is reduced.

- Work with team members or colleagues to co-create a gratitude practice at work. Involving others will make it credible and increase buy-in. Ensure you cultivate something easy to implement and reward people for keeping it up.

- Find one way you want to improve your gratitude by 1 percent. It might be a technique mentioned above, getting outside daily and appreciating nature, watching silly puppy videos, or finding gratitude in humor. Find something you love that rewards you for doing it.

Epilogue/Conclusion

▬ ▬ ▬ ▬ ▬ ▬ ▬ ▬ ▬ ▬ ▬ ▬ ▬ ▬ ▬

The concept of the endurance leader leverages a unique framework for helping the everyday leader build the mindset and behaviors to lead—and live—successfully for the long term. We live in a constantly changing and unpredictable world where stress levels are at the highest ever measured, and there is massive dissatisfaction with the world of work. As such, it may seem this book is out of step as it offers no quick fixes or simple tricks to make it all OK. It also does not engage in the kind of pop psychology self-help ("I can help you live your best life!" "I will help you uncover what's possible!") that may feel good but, like cotton candy, disappears in the span of a moment.

Instead, this four-part model (anchor your mindset, excel in execution, forge discipline, and leverage support) provides a roadmap for your leadership journey to help you manage the hills, valleys, twists and turns, bumps and summits that inevitably await. I hope this model enables you to start (or restart) your journey with the right frame of mind, provides valuable strategies you can execute, and enables you to build support to help you reach your goals.

I wish you joy in your journey and that, when you cross your leadership finish line, you will know you've given it the best of what you had and fulfilled the mission you set out for. I'll be there on the race course, cheering you on.

Appendix 1: Coaching Action Plan

Coaching Action Plan

Name: **Effective Dates:**

Focus Area #1 (list your goal, e.g., build strategic leadership capacity, enhance inter personal success at the executive level, build agility and risk-taking):

Motivation
- If I improve in this area, I will:

- If I fail to improve in this area, I will:

Success
- When I am successful, others will see:

- When I am successful, the business will experience:

- Who can help me achieve this goal?

- What resources do I need to achieve this goal?

Repeat for additional Focus Areas, if needed.

Acknowledgments

*Acknowledging the good that you already have in your life
is the foundation for all abundance.*

ECKHART TOLLE

The writing of this book is the longest endurance event I've ever embarked upon. I first jotted notes about the concept of this book in 2018, but it took me six years to complete. Life offered many twists and turns during that time, and there were several times when I couldn't see the finish line and almost gave up. But true to the words written here, there is power in leveraging support. Many people helped me return to the importance of this material and the value it could bring to the people I love working with.

As always, nothing in my life would be possible without the constant support of my husband, Dave, who has stood by me through significant intrapsychic storms and never once wavered in his commitment to helping me find a resolution to this project—one way or another. Words of gratitude will never be enough, Dave. I am thankful for you always being my selfless advocate, my biggest cheerleader, my LOML.

To the members of the Alexcel Group, particularly those who helped me give voice to this project at my first meeting in Santa Monica in 2016. Brian Underhill, you told me, "Write what you know—you know Ironman racing, write about that." Who knew that years later, we would be here? Also, I am so grateful at that meeting for former and current members Bonnie Hagemann, Carlos Paulet, Kevin Hummel, Peter Berner, Scott Eblin, Val Markos, and may their souls rest in peace, Karen Steadman, and Dirk Baxter. Thank you all for cheering me on and pushing me, even when I was still a perfect stranger.

To the other Alexcellents who not only supported my efforts but practically demanded that I "finish the damn thing already!" This includes fellow book writers Carolyn Maue, Chris Fehrnstrom, Maya Hu-Chan, Nancy Parsons, and Simon Vetter, and other committed gal pals Barb McMahon, Becky Turner, Beth Schumaker, Colleen Bastian, Danielle Vidal, and Lubna Somjee. Thank you for believing in me and being an inspiration in your own right. Joel Garfinkle, thank you for coaching me through the final edits when my soul hurt so much that I couldn't concentrate. We unwittingly put the book's concepts into practice and got this thing across the finish line. I could not have done it without you.

I am indebted to Marshall Goldsmith for taking the time to read the contents and author the book's foreword. I am grateful for your support and advocacy for this work and look forward to learning even more lessons from your coaching work. Life is good.

To my colleagues and coconspirators who continually model the way, professionally and personally. Your rock-solid values, professional commitment, and personal humility inspire and uplift me, even when the road seemed long and it was tough to run the mile I was in. These include my first and forever mentor, Bill "Dr. B" Haas, Brodie Riordan, Cedric Williams, Frank Merritt, Kathleen Gounaris, Lara Otte, Laurie Moret, Mitch Glick, Morgan Hembree, Rehman Abdulrehman, and

Susan Thornton. Thank you for your friendship, leadership by example, and unwavering support.

To my colleague, fellow Indie Books family author, and friend John O'Brien, for constantly encouraging me to finish this work and providing the perfect tweak to the book's subtitle. Kudos to you for making the notion of civility in the workplace en vogue again.

For everyone who took the time to read some or all of this book and provide me with rich and essential feedback. Your feedback truly is a gift that made this work so much better. Laurie Moret, I am forever in your debt for providing input on almost every page of the whole dang thing, and Beth Schumaker for propelling yourself through the entire missive. You two truly embody the notion of commitment. And Dave, I'll never ask whether you wanted to or felt you had to. But thank you for your handwritten input, gentle clarifications, and smiley faces on your three-inch printed copy of the manuscript.

To the endurance athletes and leaders who generously gave their time and talent, which form the backbone of this work. Your insights affirmed the relationship among these concepts and supplied meaningful, practical applicability. In particular, the endurance leaders I interviewed included Al Monserrat, Bill Parsons, Blake Snider, Clint Demetriou, Harlan Weisman, Joe Scodari, Regina Birdsell, Roger Oxendale, Stephen Murray, and Todd Briddell. I'm grateful you stuck with me even when the timeline was…a bit long. I hope I have represented you well and made you proud.

I'm grateful to my endurance athlete friends who let me poke inside their brains and watch them train to test my hypotheses. *Grazie per tutti* to the Italian Ironman power couple Alessandro Valenti and Elisabetta Villa. Additional inspirational athlete friends include Bruce and Colleen Bastian, Heike Yates, Jan Amtrup, Katie Aguilar, Kelly Sydney, Jaimie Johnson, Mark Helton, Mary Doyle, Mike McCarraher, Phyllis Ryder, Sandra Holmberg, Sean Bennett, and so many endurance athletes who also happen to work in essential jobs where they manifest the principles

216 | The Endurance Leader

outlined in this book. Whenever I refer to the section on leveraging support, you remain at the top of my mind.

To my clients, who are the true inspiration behind this work. Your rich experiences help readers connect with the essence of the endurance leader and how the concept can build a lasting, positive approach to leadership. I am humbled and honored to have the opportunity to work with you, and I admire your continued commitment and tenacity to being the best possible leaders you can be. A huge note of thanks to my coaching client, David Lee Windecher, who is loud and proud about our work together and has supported me as much as I've supported him. Thank you, my friend, for always showing up for yourself and your unwavering support of me in this effort.

I'm grateful for my original book coach, Bonnie Budzowski, one of the best unofficial psychotherapists I've encountered. Bonnie, you not only provided exceptional writing insight and direction, but you also helped me come to terms with understanding the place this book should—and shouldn't—have in my life. And you led me to Henry DeVries and Indie Books International, who helped this move from our vision to a finished product.

Thanks to the entire team at Indie Books International, firstly Henry DeVries, for welcoming me into the Indie family and helping me prioritize this writing. Thanks to Lisa Lucas and Gail Severns for their editing support and Devin Devries and Suzanne Hagen for gently pushing me to settle on a title and book cover. Thank you to the whole team for returning me to the primary goal of writing a book I'd be proud of. You truly have a family with your authors, and I am proud to be a part of that family.

To the creative people who have contributed to the artistic direction of this book, particularly Mohktar Joundi, who guided some of my original endurance leader designs. I am indebted to Melissa Farr for bringing all the images and the book cover to life. Your work to create illustrations that people could quickly identify and understand has been critical to the credibility of this work.

To my siblings and in-laws for showing up for me as I began to go public with these concepts, and a special thanks to my brother Pete for promoting these ideas to others who helped launch them into actual work. To all of you, I'm grateful for your belief in me—even when you might not always understand what I do. And for my mom, Elizabeth Evangelista, who may never get why I felt the need to author a book but loves and encourages me anyway. Still living independently and driving at ninety, you exemplify the endurance leader better than anyone I know, Mom. Keep after it.

Most importantly, I want to thank my heavenly Creator, whose love through Christ has enabled my ultimate mission. While it was my goal to create a work that can be helpful to leaders, my headstone goal is "To be loved by God and to return God's abundant love through igniting love, leadership, and service in my family, my clients, and my community." May this book be one small step in my life's journey to live the mission you have put on my heart.

About The Author

D r. Ann Bowers-Evangelista ("B-E") is a licensed clinical psychologist with an MBA and twenty-five years of experience consulting to and coaching business leaders. After a decade working for consulting psychology firms, she founded Llumos ("we light" in Latin) in 2012. Her passion for the endurance leader is borne out of her firsthand leadership experience and her longstanding experience as a triathlete, which began in 2001. Ann has completed over forty triathlons, including fifteen half-Ironman races, one full-distance Ironman race, and many shorter races. She has also completed three marathons and more half marathons than she can count, a few century rides, and some distance swim races. As the pioneer of and foremost authority on the endurance leader approach to leadership, she is a sought-after speaker and expert on this topic.

The youngest of seven children, Ann is also a proud military spouse to her active-duty husband, Colonel Dave B-E (go Air Force!). After living in Italy, Japan, and several cities in the US, Ann and Dave now happily call Washington, DC home. They spend their time in outdoor activities and working on their 1920s Craftsman home when they are too injured to train (the reality of the aging endurance athlete). They also enjoy traveling, spending time at their family lake house in the Finger Lakes of New York, and making weekly homemade pizza.

Works Cited

1 Case Western Reserve University, Weatherhead School of Management, "Five Levels of Leadership" https://weatherhead.case.edu/executive-education/programs/executive-leadership-development-experience/levels.

2 "Stress in America 2023: A Nation Recovering from Collective Trauma," American Psychological Association, November 2023, https://www.apa.org/news/press/releases/stress/2023/collective-trauma-recovery.

3 Anna Medaris, "Women say they're stressed, misunderstood, and alone," American Psychological Association, November 1, 2023, https://www.apa.org/topics/stress/women-stress.

4 Anna Medaris, "Gen Z Adults and Younger Millennials Are 'Completely Overwhelmed' by Stress," American Psychological Association, November 1, 2023, https://www.apa.org/topics/stress/generation-z-millennials-young-adults-worries?ref=theissue.io.

5 Ben Weigert, "6 Workplace Trends Leaders Should Watch in 2024," Gallup, December 18, 2023, https://www.gallup.com/workplace/547283/workplace-trends-leaders-watch-2024.aspx.

6 Gallup, "The Benefits of Employee Engagement," originally published June 20, 2013, and updated January 7, 2023. https://www.gallup.com/workplace/236927/employee-engagement-drives-growth.aspx.

7 Anna Medaris Miller, "How to Achieve Your 'Unthinkable' Fitness (and Other) Goals," *US News and World Report*, February 2, 2015, https://health.usnews.com/health-news/health-wellness/articles/2015/02/02/how-to-achieve-your-unthinkable-fitness-and-other-goals.

8 Interview with the subject, May 7, 2018.

9 Interview with the subject, July 5, 2021.

10 BJ Fogg, *Tiny Habits: The Small Changes that Change Everything* (New York: Harvest, 2020).

11 James Clear, *Atomic Habits: An Easy & Proven Way to Build Good Habits & Break Bad Ones* (New York: Random House, 2015).

12 "Our Mission," Back on My Feet, Accessed June 18, 2024, https://backonmyfeet.org/about-us/.

13 Linda Rogers, "In need of a life reboot?" The Human Performance Institute® can help. March 5, 2019, https://www.jnj.com/health-and-wellness/reboot-your-life-human-performance-institute-work-life-balance-energy-resilience-programs.

[14] Kieran Setiya, "The Midlife Crisis," University of Michigan *Philosopher's Imprint.* Creative Commons, 2014.

[15] Mary Oliver, "The Summer Day," *New and Selected Poems* (Boston: Beacon Press,1992).

[16] David Gelles, "Thasunda Brown Duckett of Chase: 'People Need to Know Who you Are,' *The New York Times*, April 4, 2019, https://www.nytimes.com/2019/04/04/business/thasunda-duckett-jpmorgan-corner-office.html.

[17] Chris Nikic, "About Chris Nikic," 2021, https://chrisnikic.com/about/.

[18] Pedro J Teixeira, Eliana V Carraça, David Markland, Marlene N Silva, and Richard M Ryan, "Exercise, physical activity, and self-determination theory: A systematic review," *The International Journal of Behavioral Nutrition and Physical Activity*, 9:(2012): 78. Doi: 10.1186/1479-5868-9-78.

[19] Richard M. Ryan and Edward L. Deci, "Self-Determination Theory and the Facilitation of Intrinsic Motivation, Social Development, and Well-Being," *American Psychologist* 55, no. 1(2000::68-73, https://psycnet.apa.org/doi/10.1037/0003-066X.55.1.68.

[20] Orhan Çınar, Çetin Bektaş, and Imran Aslan, "A Motivation Study on the Effectiveness of Intrinsic and Extrinsic Factors," *Economics and Management* 16: 690–695, May 2011, https://www.researchgate.net/publication/267711459_A_Motivation_Study_on_the_Effectiveness_of_Intrinsic_and_Extrinsic_Factors.

[21] David Giantasio, "FCB Canada Explores Fitness as a Key to Cognition for People with Down Syndrome," Muse by Clio, March 22, 2021. https://musebycl.io/sports/fcb-canada-explores-fitness-key-cognition-people-down-syndrome.

[22] T2information, "What is 360-Degree Feedback?" https://t2informatik.de/en/smartpedia/360-degree-feedback/.

[23] Natalie Komitsky, "The Johari Window, a Tool for Federal Agency Teams." Management Concepts, https://resources.managementconcepts.com/download/leadership-management/the-johari-window-model-a-tool-for-federal-agency-teams/.

[24] J.P. Flaum, "When It Comes to Business Leadership, Nice Guys Finish First," Green Peak Partners, 2010, https://greenpeakpartners.com/wp-content/uploads/2018/09/Green-Peak_Cornell-University-Study_What-predicts-success.pdf.

[25] James Clear, *Atomic Habits: An Easy & Proven Way to Build Good Habits & Break Bad Ones* (New York: Penguin Random House, 2018).

[26] Andre Adams, "Periodization Training Simplified: Your Guide to the Cycles and Phases," https://blog.nasm.org/periodization-training-simplified.

[27] Yossi Sheffi, "Preparing for disruptions through early detection," MIT Sloan Management Review, September 15, 2015 https://sloanreview.mit.edu/article/preparing-for-disruptions-through-early-detection/.

[28] Interview with the subject, June 20, 2018.

[29] Kevin Kruse, "Stephen Covey: 10 Quotes that Can Change Your Life," *Forbes*, July 16, 2012, https://www.forbes.com/sites/kevinkruse/2012/07/16/the-7-habits/.

30 BJ Fogg, "Go tiny for New Year's resolutions that work," Shareable, January 6, 2022. https://www.shareable.net/go-tiny-for-new-year-resolutions-that-work-2/.

31 "Couch to 5K in Just Six Weeks? Here's the Training Plan You've Been Looking For," *Runner's World*, updated December 19, 2023, https://www.runnersworld.com/uk/training/5km/a760067/six-week-beginner-5k-schedule/.

32 "Get Running with Couch to 5K," NHS, https://www.nhs.uk/live-well/exercise/get-running-with-couch-to-5k/.

33 "What? So What? Now What?" Reflection Toolkit, The University of Edinburgh, January 30, 2023, https://www.ed.ac.uk/reflection/reflectors-toolkit/reflecting-on-experience/what-so-what-now-what.

34 Daniel Kahneman, *Thinking, Fast and Slow* (New York: Farrar, Straus, and Giroux, 2011).

35 "Olympic Champions! Tom Daley & Matty Lee's Golden Dive," Team GB, August 14, 2022, https://www.youtube.com/watch?v=Jdk8h4fse7I.

36 Andrea Faull and Brendan Cropley, "Reflective Learning in Sport: A Case Study of a Senior Level Triathlete," *Reflective Practice* 10, no. 3 (July 14, 2009): 325–339, https://doi.org/10.1080/14623940903034655.

37 Interview with the subject, May 31, 2018.

38 Klodiana Lanaj, Trevor A. Foulk, and Amir Erez, "Energizing Leaders Via Self-Reflection: A Within-Person Field Experiment," *Journal of Applied Psychology* 104, no. 1(2019): 1–18, https://psycnet.apa.org/doi/10.1037/apl0000350.

39 James M. Citrin, Claudius A. Hildebrand, and Robert J. Stark, "The CEO Life Cycle: A Study of Performance Over Time," *Harvard Business Review*, November–December 2019, https://hbr.org/2019/11/the-ceo-life-cycle.

40 Nate Last, "Meditation for Athletes Improves Sports Performance," Mental Grit Consulting, January 3, 2017, https://www.mentalgritconsulting.com/meditation-for-athletes-improves-performance/.

41 Robb B. Rutledge, Nikolina Skandali, Peter Dayan, and Raymond J. Dolan, "A Computational and Neural Model of Momentary Subjective Well-Being," *PNAS 111*, no. 33: 12252–12257, August 4, 2014, https://doi.org/10.1073/pnas.1407535111.

42 Brad Stulberg, "How Did Veteran Endurance Athlete Rebecca Rusch Summit Mount Kilimanjaro on a Mountain Bike?" *Outside*, updated May 12, 2022, https://www.outsideonline.com/health/training-performance/how-did-veteran-endurance-athlete-rebecca-rusch-summit-mount-kilimanjaro-mountain-bike/.

43 "A Crisis Is Not a Marathon—But It Is a Call for Endurance," SmartBrief, Weaving Influence, April 16, 2020, https://www.smartbrief.com/original/2020/04/crisis-not-marathon-it-call-endurance.

44 Interview with the author, June 20, 2018.

45 Carol Dweck, "Developing a Growth Mindset with Carol Dweck," Stanford+Connects lecture, New York, Stanford Alumni Association, October 9, 2014, https://www. youtube.com/watch?v=hiiEeMN7vbQ.

46 Albert Bandura, "Self-Efficacy Mechanism in Human Agency," *American Psychologist* 37, no. 2 (1982): 122–147, https://psycnet.apa.org/doi/10.1037/0003-066X.37.2.122.

47 Sabrina Skorski and Chris R. Abbiss, "The Manipulation of Pace Within Endurance Sport," *Frontiers in Physiology* 8, no. 102, February 26, 2017, https://doi. org/10.3389%2Ffphys.2017.00102.

48 "How Katie Ledecky Changes Her Kick for Maximum Efficiency," Effortless Swimming, July 21, 2019, https://www.youtube.com/watch?v=gfnCcFQaWdU.

49 Paul Keegan, "Employees Balk at End to Remote Work: 'Going Back to the Office Is Stupid,'" *Newsweek*, April 13, 2021, https://www.newsweek.com/2021/04/30/ employees-balk-end-remote-work-going-back-office-stupid-1583059.html.

50 Kate Fodera, "Not All Is Lost: Some Businesses Are Thriving during Coronavirus (COVID-19)," IMPACT, March 31, 2020, https://www.impactplus.com/blog/ not-all-is-lost-some-businesses-are-thriving-during-covid-19.

51 David Curry, "DoorDash Revenue and Usage Statistics (2024)," Business of Apps, updated January 8, 2024, https://www.businessofapps.com/data/doordash-statistics/.

52 Ashley Mateo, "Knowing Your Heart Rate Zones Can Make You Faster—Here's How," *Runner's World*, updated August 5, 2022, https://www.runnersworld.com/beginner/ a20812270/should-i-do-heart-rate-training/.

53 Jim Purcell, "Resilience: The Key to Future Business Success," Forbes, September 14, 2020, https://www.forbes.com/sites/jimpurcell/2020/09/14/resilience-the-key-to- future-business-success/?sh=2864f49a5fde.

54 Andrew Simmons, "Training in the Grey Zone: How to Avoid the Zone 3 Plateau," TRAININGPEAKS, https://www.trainingpeaks.com/blog/training-in-the-grey- zone-how-to-avoid-the-zone-3-plateau/.

55 Brené Brown, *The Gifts of Imperfection: Let Go of Who You Think You're Supposed to Be and Embrace Who You Are* (Center City, MN: Hazelden, 2010).

56 Dennis Carey, Brian Dumaine, Michael Useem, and Rodney Zemmel, "Why CEOs Should Push Back against Short-Termism," *Harvard Business Review*, May 31, 2018, https://hbr.org/2018/05/why-ceos-should-push-back-against-short-termism.

57 Nick Busca, "Through Pain and Controversy, the 'Iron Cowboy' Chases 100 Triathlons in 100 Days," *Washington Post*, June 8, 2021, https://www.washingtonpost.com/ sports/2021/06/08/iron-cowboy-james-lawrence-100-triathlons-100-days/.

58 Kate Milsom, "Iron Cowboy Announces Retirement from Triathlon after Completing Latest Challenge," 220 Triathlon, June 18, 2021, https://www.220triathlon.com/ news/iron-cowboy-announces-retirement-from-triathlon-after-completing-latest- challenge/.

59 Rónán Doherty, Sharon M. Madigan, Alan Nevill, Giles Warrington, and Jason G. Ellis, "The Sleep and Recovery Practices of Athletes," *Nutrients* 13, no. 4: 1330, April 17, 2021, https://doi.org/10.3390/nu13041330.

60 Courtney Connley, "LeBron James reveals the nighttime routine that helps him perform at the highest level,'" CNBC Changemakers, December 23, 2018, https://www.cnbc.com/2018/12/21/lebron-james-reveals-the-nighttime-routine-that-sets-him-up-for-success.html.

61 Cheri D. Mah, Kenneth E. Mah, Eric J. Kezirian, and William C. Dement, "The Effects of Sleep Extension on the Athletic Performance of Collegiate Basketball Players," *Sleep* 34, no. 7: 943–50, July 1, 2011, https://doi.org/10.5665/SLEEP.1132.

62 Robyn Braun-Trocchio, Austin J. Graybeal, Andreas Kreutzer, Elizabeth Warfield, Jessica Renteria, Kaitlyn Harrison, Ashlynn Williams, Kamiah Moss, and Meena Shah, "Recovery Strategies in Endurance Athletes," *Journal of Functional Morphology and Kinesiology* 7, no. 1 (2022): 22. https://doi.org/10.3390/jfmk7010022.

63 John Leicester and Andres Dampf, "Osaka fined $15k for skipping French Open media; Thiem out," APnews.com, May 30, 2021, https://apnews.com/article/europe-paris-french-open-tennis-health-2808690d5309d3096355e1e2e11910b8.

64 Sara Tardiff, "Simone Biles Called Dropping Out of the Tokyo Olympics Her 'Biggest Win,'" *Teen Vogue*, April 14, 2022, https://www.teenvogue.com/story/simone-biles-called-dropping-out-of-the-tokyo-olympics-her-biggest-win.

65 "2023 Work in America Survey," American Psychological Association, https://www.apa.org/pubs/reports/work-in-america/2023-workplace-health-well-being.

66 Brenè Brown, *The Gifts of Imperfection: Let Go of Who You Think You're Supposed to Be and Embrace Who You Are*, (Center City, MN: Hazelden Publishing, 2022).

67 Michael E. Porter and Nitin Nohria, "How CEOs Manage Their Time," Harvard Business Review, July–August 2018, https://hbr.org/2018/07/how-ceos-manage-time.

68 Shawn Achor and Michelle Gielan, "The Data-Driven Case for Vacation," *Harvard Business Review*, July 13, 2016, https://hbr.org/2016/07/the-data-driven-case-for-vacation.

69 Christian D'Andrea, "Des Linden Waited for a Teammate, Almost Dropped Out Before Winning 2018 Boston Marathon," SBNation, April 16, 2018, https://www.sbnation.com/2018/4/16/17243392/des-linden-waited-teammate-bathroom-almost-dropped-out-2018-boston-marathon.

70 Kathleen Elkins, "2018 Boston Marathon Winner Des Linden Says This Key to Success Is 'Something That's Often Neglected,'" CNBC, April 13, 2019, https://www.cnbc.com/2019/04/12/des-linden-says-grit-and-mental-toughness-are-key-to-success.html.

71 Laura Williams, "Marathon Champ Des Linden's 7 Tips for Practicing Mental Toughness," Everyday Health, April 5, 2023, https://www.everydayhealth.com/emotional-health/marathon-champ-des-lindens-tips-for-practicing-mental-toughness/.

[72] Daniel Gucciardi et al., "The Concept of Mental Toughness: Tests of Dimensionality, Nomological Network, and Traitness," *Journal of Personality* 83, no. 1 (February 2015): 26–44, https://doi.org/10.1111/jopy.12079.

[73] George P. Yankov, Nicholas Davenport, and Ryne A. Sherman, "Locating Mental Toughness in Factor Models of Personality," *Personality and Individual Differences* 151 (2019), https://doi.org/10.1016/j.paid.2019.109532.

[74] Lee Crust and Peter J. Clough, "Developing Mental Toughness: From Research to Practice," *Journal of Sport Psychology in Action 2*, no. 1 (2011): 21–32, https://doi.org/10.1080/21520704.2011.563436.

[75] Brad Cooper, "Resilience, Grit & Mental Toughness: Differences and Why It Matters to You," Published on LinkedIn, November 4, 2020, https://www.linkedin.com/pulse/resilience-grit-mental-toughness-differences-why-you-cooper-phd/.

[76] Ryan Holiday in Tim Ferriss, "Stoicism 101: A Practical Guide for Entrepreneurs," *Tim Ferris* (blog), April 13, 2009, https://tim.blog/2009/04/13/stoicism-101-a-practical-guide-for-entrepreneurs.

[77] Interview with the author, June 20, 2018.

[78] Tomas Chamorro-Premuzic and Derek Lusk, "The Dark Side of Resilience," *Harvard Business Review*, August 16, 2017, https://hbr.org/2017/08/the-dark-side-of-resilience.

[79] Jennifer Moss, "The Pandemic Changed Us. Now Companies Have to Change Too." *Harvard Business Review*, July 1, 2022, https://hbr.org/2022/07/the-pandemic-changed-us-now-companies-have-to-change-too.

[80] "Good Is the Enemy of Great," Jim Collins (website), accessed March 6, 2024, https://www.jimcollins.com/media_topics/GoodIsTheEnemyOfGreat.html.

[81] Steven Krupp and Becky Hogan, "Agility for the Long Term," Heidrick & Struggles, 2021, https://www.heidrick.com/-/media/heidrickcom/publications-and-reports/agility_for_the_long_term.pdf.

[82] Michael Fitzpatrick, "How Tiger Woods' Career Might Have Turned Out Differently," Bleacher Report, February 16, 2015, https://bleacherreport.com/articles/2366463-how-tiger-woods-career-might-have-turned-out-differently.

[83] Paul MacInnes, "Chris Froome Conscious after Surgery but Rider Remains in Intensive Care," *Guardian*, June 13, 2019, https://www.theguardian.com/sport/2019/jun/13/chris-froome-intensive-care-two-three-days-after-surgery-cycling.

[84] Daniel McMahon, "Chaos Hits Tour de France as Race Leader Froome Runs Up Epic Mont Ventoux Climb After Crashing into Motorcycle and Breaking Bike," *Business Insider*, July 14, 2016, https://www.businessinsider.com/chris-froome-runs-up-ventoux-climb-tour-de-france-2016-7.

[85] Matthew Ray, "How Chris Froome Breaks Boundaries of Pro Cycling," Red Bulletin, September 11, 2017, https://www.redbull.com/gb-en/theredbulletin/how-chris-froome-is-breaking-the-boundaries-of-pro-cycling.

[86] Charles Hummel, *The Tyranny of the Urgent*, (Westmont, IL: Intervarsity Press, 1984).

[87] Ryan W. Angus, Mark D. Packard, and Brent B. Clark, "Distinguishing Unpredictability from Uncertainty in Entrepreneurial Action Theory," *Small Business Economics* 60 (July 18, 2023): 1147–1169, https://doi.org/10.1007/s11187-022-00651-4.

[88] Johnny Long, "Chris Froome: 'I've Got My Running Shoes in the Car So I'm Ready for Ventoux,'" *Cycling Weekly*, July 6, 2021, https://www.cyclingweekly.com/news/chris-froome-ive-got-my-running-shoes-in-the-car-so-im-ready-for-ventoux.

[89] Masterj328, "Michael Jordan—Nike Failure Commercial," October 8, 2009, https://www.youtube.com/watch?v=K23zLUL_6QM.

[90] Patrick Kolb, "How Michael Jordan's Mindset Made Him a Great Competitor," USA Basketball, November 24, 2015, https://www.usab.com/news/2015/11/how-michael-jordans-mindset-made-him-a-great-competitor.

[91] Mark H. Histed, Anitha Pasupathy, and Earl K. Miller, "Learning Substrates in the Primate Prefrontal Cortex and Striatum: Sustained Activity Related to Successful Actions," *Neuron* 63, no. 2 (July 30, 2009): 244–253, https://doi.org/10.1016/j.neuron.2009.06.019.

[92] Amy Edmondson and Adi Ignatius, "It's OK to Fail, But You Have to Do It Right," *Harvard Business Review*, July 28, 2023, https://hbr.org/2023/07/its-ok-to-fail-but-you-have-to-do-it-right.

[93] George Iwaki, "Final Voyage of the Challenger," Harvard Business School, November 28, 1990, http://hbr.org/product/final-voyage-of-the-challenger/an/691037-PDF-ENG.

[94] PopTech, "Benjamin Zander—PopTech 2008," September 20, 2022, https://www.youtube.com/watch?v=YRWTkQAPCAM.

[95] Amy C. Edmondson, "Strategies for Learning from Failure," *Harvard Business Review*, April 2011, https://hbr.org/2011/04/strategies-for-learning-from-failure.

[96] Kimberly Harrington, "What Is 'Toxic Positivity' and Why Is It a Problem? A New Book Explains," *Washington Post*, January 27, 2022, https://www.washingtonpost.com/books/2022/01/27/toxic-positivity-book/.

[97] Lucy McGuirk, Peter Kuppens, Rosemary Kingston, and Brock Bastian, "Does a Culture of Happiness Increase Rumination Over Failure?" *Emotion* 18, no. 5 (2018), 755–764, https://doi.org/10.1037/emo0000322.

[98] World Triathlon Corporation, Ironman U, Ironman Coaching Certification Program (website), https://u.ironman.com/courses/ironman-coaching-certification.

[99] "2020 ICF Global Coaching Study: Executive Summary," International Coaching Federation, 2020, https://coachfederation.org/app/uploads/2020/09/FINAL_ICF_GCS2020_ExecutiveSummary.pdf.

[100] Maria Kavussanu, Ian D. Boardley, Natalia Jutkiewicz, Samantha Vincent, and Christopher Ring. "Coaching efficacy and coach effectiveness: Examining their

predictors and comparing coaches' and athletes' reports," *The Sport Psychologist*, 2008, 22(4): 383-404.

[101] Sheila M. Boysen, "Coaching Effectiveness: Coach and Coachee Characteristics that Lead to Success," *Philosophy of Coaching: An International Journal* 3, no. 2 (November 2018): 6–26, http://dx.doi.org/10.22316/poc/03.2.02.

[102] Herminia Ibarra and Anne Scoular, "The Leader as Coach," *Harvard Business Review*, November-December 2019, https://hbr.org/2019/11/the-leader-as-coach.

[103] Michelle A. Barton and Kathleen M. Sutcliffe, "Enacting Resilience: Adventure Racing as a Microcosm of Resilience Organizing," *Journal of Contingencies and Crisis Management* 31, no. 3 (March 20, 2023): 560–574, https://doi.org/10.1111/1468-5973.12459.

[104] Stanford Seed, "Workplace Friction: How to Make the Right Things Easier and the Wrong Things Harder," Stanford Graduate School of Business podcast, December 13, 2023, https://www.gsb.stanford.edu/insights/workplace-friction-how-make-right-things-easier-wrong-things-harder.

[105] Matheus Honorato, "10 Has-Been Athletes with the Biggest Egos and 10 Who Have Stayed Humble," TheSportster, May 22, 2018, https://www.thesportster.com/entertainment/athletes-egos-and-the-most-humble/.

[106] Marcel Schwantes, "The World's 10 Top CEOs (They Lead in a Totally Unique Way)," Inc., March 29, 2017, https://www.inc.com/marcel-schwantes/heres-a-top-10-list-of-the-worlds-best-ceos-but-they-lead-in-a-totally-unique-wa.html.

[107] Marshall Goldsmith, "Instead of Feedback, Try Feedforward to Boost Team Performance," *Inc.*, October 21, 2014, https://www.inc.com/marshall-goldsmith/power-of-feedforward.html.

[108] ATD—Association for Training and Development, "Talent Development Glossary Terms: What Is Mentoring?" https://www.td.org/talent-development-glossary-terms/what-is-mentoring.

[109] Marshall Goldsmith, "How to Get Incredibly Helpful Feedback from Just About Anyone!" published on LinkedIn, June 20, 2017, https://www.linkedin.com/pulse/how-get-incredibly-helpful-feedback-from-just-anyone-goldsmith.

[110] Clayton M. Christiansen," How will you measure your life?" *Harvard Business Review*, July–August 2010, https://hbr.org/2010/07/how-will-you-measure-your-life.

[111] "American Born—Female African American All-Time Marathon Rankings," Black Female Marathon History, Ted Corbett Archives, March 2, 2023, https://tedcorbitt.com/black-female-marathon-history.

[112] Sika Henry, "My First Sub-3 Hour Marathon," *Why I Run* (blog), November 24, 020, https://why-i-run.blogspot.com/2020/11/my-first-sub-3-hour-marathon.html.

[113] Keith Naughton, "Ford tests buzzing wristbands to keep workers at safe distances," Bloomberg, April 15, 2020, https://www.bloomberg.com/news/articles/2020-04-15/ford-tests-buzzing-distancing-wristbands-to-keep-workers-apart#xj4y7vzkg.

[114] Marian N. Ruderman and Cathleen Clerkin, "Is the Future of Leadership Development Wearable? Exploring Self-Tracking in Leadership Programs," *Industrial and Organizational Psychology* 13, no. 1 (May 1, 2020): 103–116, https://doi.org/10.1017/iop.2020.18.

[115] Robert Feldmar, "The Rise of the Smartwatch: Will Smartphones Become Redundant?" Resco, August 12, 2020, https://www.resco.net/blog/smartwatch-will-smartphones-become-redundant/.

[116] Megan Reitz and John Higgins, "How AI Features Can Change Team Dynamics," *Harvard Business Review*, April 1, 2024, https://hbr.org/2024/04/how-ai-features-can-change-team-dynamics.

[117] Thomas Watson, updated by Ben Gibbons, "Rate of Perceived Exertion: Why RPE Is the Best Running Metric," Marathon Handbook, updated January 17, 2024, https://marathonhandbook.com/rate-of-perceived-exertion/.

[118] Mike Plant, "Legend: The Always-Smiling Chrissie Wellington," *Triathlete*, updated January 31, 2020, https://www.triathlete.com/culture/legend-the-always-smiling-chrissie-wellington.

[119] Chrissie Wellington, *A Life Without Limits: A World Champion's Journey* (New York: Hachette Book Group, 2012), 20.

[120] John C. Maxwell (@johncmaxwell), "Gratitude is one of the most important components of leadership, and it's essential for lifetime growth. Remember this: What we appreciate appreciates, and what we depreciate depreciates!" Instagram, July 29, 2023, https://www.instagram.com/p/CvSkv8kxY9t/.

[121] Imed Bouchirka, "35 Scientific Benefits of Gratitude: Mental Health Research Findings in 2024," Research.com, February 8, 2024, https://research.com/education/scientific-benefits-of-gratitude.

[122] Nicole T. Gabana, Jesse A. Steinfeldt, Y. Joel Wong, and Y. Berry Chung, "Gratitude, Burnout, and Sport Satisfaction Among College Student-Athletes: The Mediating Role of Perceived Social Support," *Journal of Clinical Sport Psychology* 11, no. 1 (2017): 14–33, https://doi.org/10.1123/jcsp.2016-0011.

[123] Lung Hung Chen, Chia-Huei Wu, and Jen-Ho Chang, "Gratitude and Athletes' Life Satisfaction: The Moderating Role of Mindfulness," Journal of Happiness Studies 18 (June 10, 2017): 1147–1159, https://doi.org/10.1007/s10902-016-9764-7.

[124] Laura S. Redwine, Brook L. Henry, Meredith A. Pung, Kathleen Wilson, Kelly Chinh, Brian Knight, Shamini Jain, Thomas Rutledge, Berry Greenberg, Alan Maisel, and Paul J. Mills, "Pilot Randomized Study of a Gratitude Journaling Intervention on Heart Rate Variability and Inflammatory Biomarkers in Patients with Stage B Heart Failure," *Psychosomatic Medicine* 78, no. 6 (July–Aug 2016): 667–676, https://doi.org/10.1097/psy.0000000000000316.

[125] Kirsten Weir, "Employees Really Value Making a Difference at Work. Here Are 7 Tips from Psychology to Get Them There," American Psychological Association, July 13, 2023, https://www.apa.org/topics/healthy-workplaces/making-difference-at-work.

126 Ricky N. Lawton, Julian Gramatki, Will Watt, and Daniel Fujisawa, "Does Volunteering Make Us Happier, or Are Happier People More Likely to Volunteer? Addressing the Problem of Reverse Causality When Estimating the Wellbeing Impacts of Volunteering," *Journal of Happiness Studies* 22 (March 17, 2020): 599–624, https://doi.org/10.1007/s10902-020-00242-8.

127 Angela Thoresen, "Helping People, Changing Lives: 3 Health Benefits of Volunteering," Mayo Clinic, August 1, 2023, https://www.mayoclinichealthsystem.org/hometown-health/speaking-of-health/3-health-benefits-of-volunteering.

128 Yun Geng, Yafan Chen, Chienchung Huang, Huanfa Tan, Congcong Zhang, and Shaoming Zhu, "Volunteering, Charitable Donation, and Psychological Well-Being of College Students in China," *Frontiers in Psychology* 12 (January 6, 2022): 790528, https://doi.org/10.3389/fpsyg.2021.790528.

Printed in Great Britain
by Amazon

50993412R00138